SELECTING AND MANAGING ELECTRONIC RESOURCES

A How-To-Do-It Manual for Librarians

Revised Edition

Vicki L. Gregory
with assistance by
Ardis Hanson

HOW-TO-DO-IT MANUALS FOR LIBRARIANS

NUMBER 146

NEAL-SCHUMAN PUBLISHERS, INC.
New York, London

Published by Neal-Schuman Publishers, Inc.
100 William Street, Suite 2004
New York, NY 10038

Printed and bound in the United States of America.

The paper used in this publication meets the minimum requirements of American National Standard for Information Sciences—Permanence of Paper for Printed Library Materials. ANSI Z39.48-1992. ∞

Library of Congress Cataloging-in-Publication Data

Gregory, Vicki L., 1950-
    Selecting and managing electronic resources : a how-to-do-it manual for librarians / Vicki L. Gregory.— Rev. ed. / with assistance by Ardis Hanson.
        p. cm. — (How-to-do-it manuals for librarians ; no. 146)
    Includes bibliographical references and index.
    ISBN 1-55570-548-0 (alk. paper)
    1. Libraries—Special collections—Electronic information resources. 2. Electronic information resources—Management. 3. Selection of nonbook materials. 4. Acquisition of electronic information resources. 5. Digital libraries—Collection development. 6. Copyright and electronic data processing—United States. 7. Digital preservation. I. Hanson, Ardis. II. Title. III. How-to-do-it manuals for libraries ; no. 146.

Z692.C65G74 2006
025.2'84—dc22
                                                    2005027888

CONTENTS

LIST OF FIGURES

PREFACE

Building a library collection today requires a high tolerance level for continuous change combined with clearheaded recognition of the need for constant evaluation and reevaluation. This situation has not always been the case. For most libraries throughout the twentieth century, the process of collecting print materials became standardized slowly and then evolved gradually. Over the last 25 years, however, the revolution of electronic resources changed the entire process. As user needs grew, resources changed. To meet user needs today, libraries must now purchase and maintain significant electronic resources. They must also offer the necessary hardware and software to make these resources accessible to users, both on-site and remotely from the user's home or office. Trying to meet this demand has severely affected the budgets of most libraries.

This revised edition of *Selecting and Managing Electronic Resources: A How-To-Do-It Manual for Librarians* recognizes that librarians today need a somewhat different expertise in order to select and evaluate electronic resources. In addition to the subject-matter knowledge used with print materials, now the selector must also have sufficient technical expertise (or have access to those with technical expertise) in order to evaluate any new resources and to analyze how well the product performs.

In the era of hard copy, paper-only resources, libraries could measure their collections in terms of feet (or miles) of shelf. Now, it is more accurate to measure a collection as a combination of resources that are physically present and the degree of access provided to electronic resources. However, even in a new electronic age, collection development librarians must still be able to identify, locate, and organize all materials so users can find the information that they need or desire.

In this regard, the basic steps of collection development remains fundamentally the same:

1. contemplate the information needs of users,
2. consider the value and extent of the existing library collection,
3. take into account available information resources,
4. determine which resources will best meet the information needs of the library's users, and
5. add the most suitable candidates to the collection.

Over the course of this electronic revolution, the library community has waited for the imminent and permanent change promised: Paper would become obsolete as collections were converted into purely electronic resources. Sometime soon there would be no need to maintain nonarchival print resources because "everything" would be available in the form of an electronic publication. Nonetheless, we still remain a considerable distance from this system.

In the early years of the revolution, some librarians treated the new electronic resources almost as fads, and some even felt safe ignoring the Internet. At that time, users were only just becoming computer-literate and Web-savvy. As their skills increased, users placed significant pressure on libraries to provide more electronic products and services. Today, it is clearly no longer possible for electronic resources to be considered "optional" collection enhancements or luxuries. Indeed, while not displacing print and hard copy to a significant degree outside of certain fields, they are fast becoming essential mainstays of almost every library's collection.

Today's electronic information arena involves resources covering a wide variety of materials, including:

- indexing and abstracting services,
- electronic books and serials,
- electronic databases offered by information aggregators,
- document delivery services, and
- Web sites.

In fact, the Internet now provides a viable alternative to the acquisition of many resources that would traditionally have been owned and housed locally. For many publications, the Internet has become the primary stimulant driving migration from print to electronic form. The Web has also solved many distribution and access problems by eliminating the need for vendors to develop and distribute proprietary software in order for clients to access their resources. Whatever money the Web saved for libraries, vendors soon realized that their losses to the Internet and to hard-copy sales could be lucratively replaced by the licensing approach, thus keeping the pressure on the libraries' budgets.

The issues involving around electronic resources are constantly changing and can rarely be resolved permanently. How does the librarian best establish and apply appropriate criteria to determine the quality and value of a particular electronic resource for a particular collection? When the integration of electronic resources results in the transformation of library services and functions, how does one deal with the many departmental barriers between the public and technical sides that now perform cross-functionally? I have revised *Selecting and Managing Electronic Resources* because these issues and many others like them continue to challenge providers of information.

ORGANIZATION

Chapter 1, "Collection Development Policies," deals with collection guidelines that are either specifically dedicated to electronic resources or that make adequate provisions for them. In the 1970s, most libraries established written collection development policies for their print collections that include some appended audiovisual materials. Today, electronic resources have become such an integral part of an institution's resources that many libraries amend and rewrite significant portions of their policies addressing electronic resources. Many larger libraries have moved toward subject-based policies in place of one overall integrated policy.

Chapter 2, "Selection Criteria and the Selection Process," opens with a discussion of needs assessment: how to determine which electronic resources are required and which available format of those resources will best meet the needs of users. This chapter explores how to utilize the best selection processes by:

- establishing reliable criteria, even for "free" Internet resources, to ensure that standards of authoritativeness and accuracy have been applied (and not just that the price was right);
- making the most of new selection methods, including trial offers, demonstrations, and visits to libraries that already own or license the particular resource; and
- creating and using selection teams.

Chapter 3, "Budgeting and Acquisitions," explores key issues involved with these two crucial areas of selecting electronic resources, including price comparisons and the effects of bundling.

Chapter 4, "Organization and Access to Electronic Resources," deals with cataloging and other tools of bibliographic control. As with print resources, once an electronic information resource is selected, the library must provide some organized method of making its users aware of the resource and how to access it. This chapter, written by Ardis Hanson, is a complete update of the previous edition; it surveys the various ways to retrieve organized materials and the common tools for accomplishing the task.

Chapter 5, "Evaluation and Assessment," examines how to determine the effectiveness of a library's mix of electronic and printed resources. It discusses techniques and points out a number of areas in which data is needed to evaluate a resource successfully.

Chapter 6, "Digital Rights Management and Intellectual Property," looks at how electronic resources have heightened libraries' concerns regarding digital rights management, copyright, and licensing for libraries; it covers some of the issues concerning copying and reproducing work. Another important area addressed is ownership versus licensing of resources, with the implications for possible restrictions on the fair use rights of users. It discusses the components of DRM (digital rights management) systems as well as issues surrounding their use as DRM becomes ubiquitous in the administration of licensed materials.

Chapter 7, "Preservation Issues," examines some of the most pressing concerns that libraries have for how to protect and offer continued access to electronic materials. How can one be confident in the life span and continued availability of electronic materials to substitute them for print materials? Is it wise to continue print subscriptions for items also being purchased in electronic format? When is the expense justified and when is it clearly wasteful? Are there any guarantees that digital materials will be updated or migrated to current operating systems and formats?

Chapter 8, "The Future of Selecting and Managing Electronic Resources," discusses developments in the selection process, and integration resources, as well as how to handle the stress of change.

The "Selected Bibliography" groups sources by subject area for the reader interested in additional information. Most, but not all, of the sources from the first edition are included, and supplementary, more up-to-date resources have been added.

The selection and management of electronic resources remains a relatively new area challenging many libraries, one that was not envisioned as a major issue when some of today's practicing librarians attended library school. For those newer to the profession, this area has always been a constant yet growing landscape. I hope that this revised edition of *Selecting and Managing Electronic Resources: A How-To-Do-It Manual for Librarians* helps some colleagues find their way and encourages others to blaze new trails.

1 COLLECTION DEVELOPMENT POLICIES

Collection development policies are really best viewed as blueprints for the operations of a library as a whole, for it is through these policies that the library carries out its central tasks of acquiring, organizing, and maintaining library materials. Collection development policies also typically set up the general framework for establishing the library's collection goals, in terms of both new acquisitions and the maintenance of existing items in the library's collections. Usually written and developed by libraries with two audiences in mind—the library's staff members and the broader community of the library's patrons and other users—collection development policies certainly vary greatly as a result. In most libraries, however, what we find today consists of a combination of descriptions of practices, guidelines for decisions, and provisions intended to protect against unwarranted pressures to acquire, to eschew the acquisition of, or to discard certain types of materials or particular items.

Collection development policies help to ensure consistency in procedures and are also important in achieving appropriate balance in a library's collection. This need for consistency exists because selectors, in using and revising the policies, are necessarily forced to confront the overall goals and objectives of the library and to reflect these goals and objectives in the collection they are building, whether that collection is owned and housed locally in hard copy form or in an electronic format or is simply accessed through the Web. Of course, proper collection balance does not mean that all areas must receive equal coverage, but rather that the collection reflect the proper balance necessary to meet the needs of the particular library's users. This touchstone remains as valid in the electronic arena as it has always been in the traditional print environment.

The rapid infusion into the stream of materials available for library acquisition of all manners and types of electronic resources (including electronic journals, databases, image collections, maps, encyclopedias, stock market reports, and other business and financial information) has, as might be expected, often strained the old rules and guidelines typically contained in traditional collection development policies. For instance, what constitutes the library's "collection"? Is it simply those items that are purchased

According to Paula Kaufman, "Librarians add credibility and validation to the collections they build, and this validation is becoming increasingly important in cyberspace, where anyone can publish anything."
—Paula T. Kaufman, "Whose Good Old Days are These? A Dozen Predictions for the Digital Age," *Journal of Library Administration* v. 35, no. 3 (2001).

and housed locally or does it include licensed materials that are housed on a server at the vendor's site? Should the library collection be considered to include materials that are freely available on the Internet? These and similar basic philosophical issues must be resolved before a successful collection development policy for electronic resources can be written today. Only when these issues are resolved will the library be ready to write or revise its current policy to take electronic materials adequately into account.

Three approaches to considering the acquisition or retention of electronic resources pursuant to libraries' collection development policies have typically been taken:

- Making electronic resources acquisitions fit into the patterns of traditional policies.
- Creating separate policies dealing only with electronic resources.
- Mainstreaming electronic resources into a reworked, integrated collection development policy. Larger libraries are now starting to do subject-specific integrated policies.

As will be seen in the following discussion, only the third approach is likely to be truly successful. Electronic resources are indubitably here to stay in one form or another, and, as time goes on, these resources will doubtless come to represent a larger portion and more important component of a typical library's collection, both in terms of number of items and expenditures. For this, if no other reason, it is vital that electronic resources be included in the overall collection plans of any library and not ignored or simply addressed separately.

TRADITIONAL POLICIES

Traditional collection development policies have typically served a number of purposes, some of which have the effect of informing and directing library processes in acquiring and making resources available to users, and some of which have served as a protection for the library against challenges to its procedures and resources. These purposes—**informing**, **directing**, and **protecting**—can be accomplished or carried out in many ways through a traditional collection development policy. To carry out the **informing** and **directing** purposes, a traditional collection development policy typically contains provisions intended to:

- Describe the library's user community, defining the institutional mission of the library, and identifying its users' likely needs.
- Provide selection criteria and guidelines for the use of those charged with selecting library materials.
- Identify those selection tools and processes that are most appropriate for the particular library.
- Define the process for identifying materials for weeding, cancellation, storage, and replacement of materials.
- Facilitate consistency and communication among the library's collection development librarians.
- Establish who is responsible for various aspects of the collection development process and collection management activities.
- Create a plan for the future of the collection and the budgeting of resultant library expenditures.
- Serve as a training document for new collection development librarians and those charged with management of the library as a whole.
- Provide guidelines for dealing with gift materials.
- Provide guidelines for dealing with complaints about materials or services thought by patrons or administrators to be inappropriate.
- Provide a framework and context for decisions concerning library access, space allocations, budgeting, and fund-raising priorities.
- Support cooperative collection development activities by discipline, documenting what the library has done in the past and what the library is currently doing with collecting levels.
- Identify both the strengths and the relative weaknesses of the library's current collections.
- Aid in preparing grant proposals and planning development initiatives through its supporting documentation.
- Serve as a communication vehicle with the library's staff, administration, and its various constituencies.

A good collection development policy will carry out its **protecting** purposes by containing provisions in such areas as:

- Protecting intellectual freedom.
- Informing the library's governing and/or funding body concerning the library's current direction.
- Providing a clear and carefully described rationale for the library's collection goals and practices.

- Making clear the principles under which decisions are made to protect the library against charges of bias and irresponsible behavior.
- Protecting the library from pressures to acquire or provide access to inappropriate or irrelevant resources.
- Acting as an informational tool for use within the library's user/patron community and for its community at large.
- Providing some protection to the library, when budgets decrease and/or materials costs increase, against complaints by the user community.

An examination of the purposes of the traditional library collection development policy reveals that virtually every one of the issues remains present and important, perhaps to a greater or lesser degree, when dealing with electronic resources. But a number of additional different and unique concerns also exist. A collection development policy that is intended to encompass electronic resources can successfully do so only if it seeks to address the issues of:

- Cancellation or retention of print resources when an electronic version of the resource becomes available.
- Provision of or limitations on remote access to electronic resources owned or licensed by the library.
- Justification of new costs, which may include the costs of hardware and supplies in addition to the cost of the material.
- Location of resources and the cost of maintaining appropriate Internet or other network links.
- Possible duplication of certain e-journals or databases, based on purchasing bundles available from different electronic information aggregators.
- Negotiation of the terms of licenses for use of the material, including provisions addressing these new types of legal considerations in the collection development policy itself.
- Consideration of the special preservation and long-term access issues that electronic resources present.
- Satisfaction by the library of the technical requirements for access to the resource, including such matters as determining the formats and computer platforms supported by the materials.
- Cancellation problems, which include whether the library loses all rights to materials previously licensed once cancellation occurs.

- Performance questions, such as whether the electronic product really performs its intended job better (that is, whether it makes information more easily or accurately available than its print counterpart).
- Training of staff and users in the use of the particular new electronic resource.
- Access and organizational issues concerning whether to catalog Internet-available items or electronic bundles of resources.
- Cooperative collection development issues, such as the ability to provide copies on interlibrary loan.

These issues and concerns make it clear that a collection development policy written purely for or with only the print environment in mind will not be of much use in the selection and management of electronic resources. Therefore, hard as it may be to do, the old policies are best discarded in favor of new approaches that keep the goals of those policies alive while simultaneously reflecting the realities of the electronic information environment.

SEPARATE POLICIES

When conventional collection development policies are perceived as having become inadequate in resolving the issues that typically revolve around electronic resources, many libraries have resorted to the development of a separate collection development policy specifically intended to cover the acquisition and maintenance of electronic resources. In some ways these "separate" policies are not that much different from the traditional approaches. For example, a separate policy might be developed for the selection of CD-ROM products; it might generally follow the basic philosophies of the library's traditional collection development policy, but supplement it by adding appropriate guidelines in respect of such matters as:

- Keeping the selection of CD-ROMs consistent with general collection development policies.
- Evaluating the searching and system capabilities (such as Boolean searching, response time, and downloading capability) of the CD-ROM product, in addition to evaluating its informational content.

- Evaluating CD-ROM vendors in terms of reliability and support as well as the validity of the informational content of their products.
- Determining the administrative costs associated with the CD-ROM product in addition to other related costs, such as those for hardware upgrades, additional disk space requirements, maintenance, and security.
- Evaluating the amount of instructional time required for staff and users to learn how to use the product effectively.
- Updating procedures, including new ones for determining whether years for the product are "rolled-off," thereby resulting in loss of coverage for earlier years.
- Networking requirements/costs for the CD-ROM product.

The separate policy approach can work, but usually only if the library has plans to obtain a limited amount of electronic information products. Thus, as more and more electronic products are purchased or licensed, the need for an integrated policy quickly becomes more apparent. First of all, if the policy is to work well, all of the library's collection development librarians will typically have to be involved to some extent in the selection of electronic resources. A separate policy approach, which tends to label these resources as "special" or different from print resources at a time when a mix of electronic and print resources is fast becoming the norm throughout all areas in the library, will quickly become inadequate. Also, to isolate the decisions regarding print and electronic resources is to invite massive duplication. If the decision-making process is integrated, and it should be, it seems logical for the collection development policy to be integrated as well. On balance then, separate collection development policies for electronic resources should be avoided. Figure 1-1 sets forth resources and examples useful in developing collection policies.

INTEGRATED POLICIES

OVERALL INTEGRATED POLICIES

Integrating electronic resources into the library's overall collection development policy has many advantages. Perhaps foremost among these advantages is that integration allows electronic resources to be placed into the plan for the overall goals of the library so that they may take their rightful place in the collection as an integral part of the library's materials in a given subject

---

**Figure 1-1: Resources and Examples to Assist in the
Development of an Integrated or Separate Electronic Collection Development Policy**

Comprehensive Sites

Arizona Department of Library, Archives and Public Records. "Collection Development Training for Arizona Public Libraries." *www.dlapr.lib.az.us/cdt/index.htm*

Acceptable Use Policies

American Library Association. "Guidelines and Consideration for Developing a Public Library Internet Use Policy." *www.ala.org/Template.cfm?Section=otherpolicies&Template=/Content Management/ContentDisplay.cfm&ContentID=13098*

Carnegie Library of Pittsburgh. "Internet Access Policies." *www.clpgh.org/clp/policy/*

University of Iowa Libraries. Acceptable Use of Information Technology Resources." *www.uiowa.edu/~our/opmanual/ii/19.htm*

Separate Policies

University of Oregon Libraries. "Electronic Journals." *libweb.uoregon.edu/colldev/cdpolicies/ejournals.html*

University of Wyoming Libraries. "Collection Development Policy on Internet Resources." *www-lib.uwyo.edu/cdo/cp_internet.htm*

Integrated Policies

Florida Atlantic University Libraries. "Collection Development Policy: FAU Libraries." *www.library.fau.edu/policies/cd_fau.htm*

Morton Grove Public Library. "Collection Development and Materials Selection Policy." *www.webrary.org/inside/colldevintro.html*

Subject-Specific Integrated Policies

LSU Libraries. "Business: Collection Development Policy Statement." *www.lib.lsu.edu/collserv/colldev/policies/business.html*

area. This process naturally leads to a unity of resources and avoids the potentially unfocused groupings of electronic materials at various "spots." This is particularly important for selectors who may otherwise miss or generally be unaware of important electronic resources within their respective specialties. Indeed, the role of the selectors remains critical, and the collection development policy should be designed first and foremost to help them do their jobs.

Important considerations for any integrated collection development policy include:

- Provisions allowing selectors to learn about and see which electronic resources would fill gaps in their library's current print collection.
- Provisions for the inclusion of prescriptive information regarding the various selection tools that review electronic resources (tools that might not initially be familiar to all selectors).
- Allowance for a more rational approach to funding the purchase of resources, both print and electronic, when viewed as a whole.
- Provision of help to library administrators and staff when challenged by users who may resist the inclusion in the collection of new and inherently expensive electronic resources.
- Allowance for more flexibility regarding new formats and types of resources.
- Encouragement of collection development across formats.

Of course, fully integrating electronic resources into a library's collection development policy means that selection criteria that pertain to electronic materials and discussion of issues particular, if not peculiar, to electronic resources must be added, wherever appropriate and needed, to the library's collection development policy. Some issues that will always need to be addressed or included in a properly integrated collection development policy are:

- Licensing issues, such as the number of users allowed at one time, remote access availability, and methods by which interlibrary loans or sharing of resources may be allowed. (See Chapter 6 for additional information concerning licensing.)
- Selection tools for electronic resources (see Chapter 2). This information should include whether selectors will only use selection tools or whether attempts will be made to identify reliable sources from Web searching.

- Selection criteria (see Chapter 2) that affect electronic resources only, such as ease of use, searching capability, operating system platform and system hardware requirements, ease of downloading, and printing capabilities.
- Selection by the item or by collection of resources (such as a Web site containing lists of links) or both.
- Access issues, such as the addition of metadata with or without full MARC cataloging of Internet resources, or a "Webliography," or a list of links on the library's Web site, or some combination of these approaches. Depending on the level of effort needed to maintain the collection of available Internet resources, stability of those resources may be a problem, but they should not be ignored for that reason alone.
- Selection issues. When the same resources can be acquired in various formats and versions, which one will be selected? If an e-journal lacks advertisements, pictorial elements, and the like, should it be considered as if it were exactly the same resource as the print journal? How is the librarian to decide whether the missing elements are important enough to warrant duplication of the item in the collection?
- Access versus ownership issues. Does the library prefer to own physical copies of resources regardless of form, when that is an option, or is access alone sufficient to meet the library's needs?
- Preservation issues. (See Chapter 7 for additional information concerning preservation issues.) Will the material be available for future users? This area includes issues of whether the library has the right to access a source over the long term (see Chapter 7) and whether the material will continue to be maintained in a format that will allow the user to access the material.
- Duplication/overlap issues between print and electronic resources, as well as duplication of electronic materials licensed in bundles from aggregators.
- Potential changes in the selection process, such as committee versus individual selection (see Chapter 2).
- Technical concerns in regard to staff and patron training, technical support, ease of installation, and technical compatibility with the library's existing hardware and software platform.
- For materials accessed remotely, availability and reliability of telecommunications, system servers, and the like.

SUBJECT-SPECIFIC INTEGRATED POLICIES

A subset of the overall integrated approach is a collection development policy that is integrated, but subject-specific. Instead of trying to devise an overall policy that fits every subject area or discipline collected by the library, separate policies are written for each subject instead of a separate policy by format. Separating policies by subject allows the writers to clearly delineate the scope and characteristics of a particular subject area. Therefore, a policy for history could look very different from one for the biological sciences. These kinds of policies allow for much more detail and generally are more helpful for both librarians and users.

Although the subject-specific policy requires many of the same elements as a broad overall collection development policy, it must also address coordination among the different subject specialties that may border on the particular policy being written. Scholarship has become much more interdisciplinary, so the policy should provide for some level of coordination with other subject areas to avoid unnecessary duplication or gaps in the collection.

The subject-specific approach can be quite useful in large libraries, but would be problematic in a small library unless specifically adapted to the particular library. For example, they might lump all the humanities, the social sciences, and the physical/biological sciences into three subject-specific policies.

The rapid nature of change associated with information technology calls for today's libraries to have collection development policies that are more flexible than those that have typically been used in the past. Libraries need policies that can encompass all the available formats of information resources, including both locally owned resources and resources that can be accessed remotely on the World Wide Web. An integrated collection development policy—either a broad overall policy or a subject-specific policy—is, it must be concluded, the best approach to take.

INTERNET RESOURCES

With the emergence and tremendous growth of the World Wide Web, there are now a multitude of essentially free resources that can be accessed by any library's users. Every day, more government documents and scholarly publications are being made available on the Web, and sometimes they are available in Web format only. Thus, another important consideration for many libraries is the question of ownership as opposed to providing only remote access to electronically available publications. Remote access to Internet or Web-based resources certainly allows for much wider access and potentially greater ease of use by the library patron, and perhaps results in lower local maintenance costs for upgrading, storing, and troubleshooting than are typical for electronic resources purchased for local use.

When the library is selecting nonproprietary Internet resources, several additional factors will need to be taken into account and a number of special issues should be considered:

1. Selection and accessibility, as opposed to collecting/purchasing.

    The Internet is a big place. What tools and how much time will selectors use to locate Internet resources to add to the library collection? It is all too easy to get engrossed with Web searching to the detriment of other duties.

2. Space and cost restrictions generally do not apply.

    Without such factors as space and cost to consider, new selection criteria must aid selectors in choosing one resource over a similar one of the same level of reliability and accuracy.

3. New types of materials can be "collected."

    Items which may have once seemed too ephemeral or fragile for the library's collection may now be "collected" on the Web.

4. Access to dynamic rather than static resources.

    The content of Web sites selected for inclusion may changes from day to day. Consider the implications of having selected materials that may change radically over time and may suddenly include materials that your community might find objectionable.

5. Resources are more likely than the corresponding printed resources to be examined as a whole.

    Web and Internet materials will probably need to be more thoroughly examined before selection than print materials presently are, simply because without examination on screen, it is usually difficult to determine ease of use problems, etc.

6. Multiple user access.

    Instead of having one copy of an item that only one

user may access at a time, the Web allows for multiple simultaneous uses of a resource.

7. Accessibility and stability of the resources.
   Is the material selected on a site that is stable in terms of its Web address? Is it accessible without too many server problems or does it require extensive amounts of time to download?

All these issues need to be addressed in the library's collection development policy if it is to be successful.

ACCEPTABLE USE POLICIES

Acceptable use policies may constitute a needed appendix to a library's collection development policy if the library offers unlimited Internet access as part of its electronic resource collection. Public libraries may find it particularly important to include appropriate online behavior rules in order to help protect children and to avoid offending other users. Of course, library policy and patron education can highlight many practical suggestions in this regard, but it should be clear that the ultimate responsibility for enforcement remains with the patron, or in the case of children, with a parent or guardian. Another area that an acceptable use policy should address is that of copyright violation or other misuse of electronic resources. (See Chapter 6 for more on copyright issues.) A number of libraries have found it appropriate to place their acceptable use policies on the Web. The American Library Association Web site contains the document "Guidelines and Considerations for Developing a Public Library Internet Use Policy" (*www.ala.org/alaorg/oif/internet.html*), which can be very helpful as a model when writing such a policy.

REVISION OF COLLECTION DEVELOPMENT POLICIES

Just as with their traditional print collection counterparts, collection development policies that include electronic materials need to be revised regularly. Furthermore, since the world of electronic resources is changing so rapidly, with new products and formats emerging almost daily, these policies probably require revision more often, and certainly require more attention or tending to than the collection development policies with which libraries typically operated in the past. Although a good collection development policy has always required careful attention to the problem of needed revisions, today's and tomorrow's information environment will make a dynamic collection development policy a necessity if the policy is to be of any real use to the library and its user community. Although the frequency and manner in which policies are revised will naturally be affected by the library's size and staff, a regular revision schedule that works well for the particular library's situation needs to be planned for and followed.

CONCLUSION

If a library has not already arrived at the happy stage in its development where there exist sufficient electronic resources available within its collection (whether physically owned or licensed for remote access or selected from free Internet resources), in all probability a new, integrated collection development policy will be needed in the near future. Electronic resources are becoming too pervasive to be relegated to "special" policies aimed at treating the new formats as something supplemental to the library's basic mission. Instead, electronic resource selection and management issues should be added to the library's current collection development policy so that emphasis can be placed on the needed or desired subject content rather than on the forms that content might take. All of the library's selectors, in every subject area of the collection or specialization of mission, will need to consider the addition of electronic resources in connection with other decisions made for the selection and acquisition of new books, serials, and audiovisual materials of all types. As with all collection development decisions, electronic resources require that a coherent rationale be established for the acquisition of each item. Then, once obtained, the electronic resource must be made available in an orderly manner with proper training for staff and users.

2 SELECTION CRITERIA AND THE SELECTION PROCESS

Before beginning the selection process itself in respect of any potential resource, it is imperative for the librarian to consider the needs of his or her library's user community. If librarians are to address successfully the many challenges presented and the opportunities that are now available through the provision and proliferation of electronic information sources, they must start from a clear understanding of their library's basic missions and goals. This is a basic necessity in order to establish the types and kinds of library resources and services that libraries should be offering to their users. As electronic resources are added to their collections, few libraries are likely to be sufficiently prosperous to continue to maintain both their prior levels of acquisition of traditional print materials and the simultaneous acquisition of the newer, electronic forms of materials. The selection decisions a library must make therefore necessarily involve a form of intellectual triage. Deciding which items to cut and which items to keep is a process best grounded on a philosophical basis, determined by a needs assessment project appropriate to the library involved, rather than on the ad hoc, item-by-item basis that is all too often utilized by many libraries.

Conducting a needs assessment project does not have to be a daunting task. The traditional journalist's approach to writing a news column by determining **who, what, when, where,** and **how** constitutes an altogether appropriate, easy to apply methodology for analyzing the measures on which to build a philosophically grounded collection needs assessment. Under this approach, you, as the librarian, need to consider:

- **Who**
  Who are the users of your library? Has your base of library users changed recently or is it likely to change as a result of adding electronic resources? If electronic resources and services are provided through the library's Web site, who is permitted to use these resources? For instance, may anyone with access to the library's Internet site use your electronic reference service or may only bona fide mem-

bers of your institutional community do so? (For example, are only the faculty and staff of a particular school or university permitted to have access?) The answers to these questions will go a considerable distance toward determining an appropriate selection approach for your library, because they affect both the quality and the quantity of the resources needed.

- **What**
  What materials or information does your library's typical user usually need or ask for? What are the apparently unmet needs of your library's current and anticipated potential users? Digging a little deeper, what do they *really* want or need (as opposed to what they say they want or need)? Is there a demand for new services, and what new services do your users need? Can electronic access to resources (both in terms of staff and text) help to provide or facilitate the provision of such services? What level of computer expertise do your library's current and expected future users have? What is the potential usage level—that is, how many users do you anticipate will want access to the same resources at the same time or at the same location?

- **When**
  When will your library's users get the materials and information they want? Or, more important, how long are your users willing to wait for resources? The spread of the electronic information environment has undoubtedly decreased the length of time most users are willing to wait for needed information. Simultaneously, the likely level of their ire when that length of time is exceeded has apparently risen exponentially. Access to electronic resources can, therefore, provide greater user satisfaction, since electronic resources usually don't circulate and are never at the bindery.

- **Where**
  Once specific materials are identified, from what location does your library's users typically need to be able to access these materials? Do they prefer to use the resource only in the library or do they want or need remote access to the item? Do users want the library to deliver documents electronically or are your users content for the electronic resource simply to direct them to a hard-copy source?

- **How**

  How can your library best obtain the information that is requested or needed? A mixture of qualitative and quantitative measures that brings in the views of a cross-section of potential users is a good approach to determining the answer to this question. The library could conduct focus group interviews with users and potential users to obtain information about user preferences, fears, and unmet needs in relation to information in general and electronic resources in particular. The library could also conduct a survey, using a mailed or electronically delivered questionnaire, or utilizing telephone inquiries or face-to-face interviews with a random or purposefully selected sample of the library's current or potential user community. These survey methods could then be supplemented with system statistics for those electronic resources your library already owns, as well as reference or interlibrary loan requests that have historically been required in order to acquire access to materials from outside the library so as to meet patron needs. Your integrated library system may allow you to gather data concerning the current use of electronic resources, the number of users of these resources, the number of searches they typically conduct (and, more important, the number of successful searches), how electronic resources are usually accessed (in-house or remotely), the number of print commands issued, and a host of other report data that will assist you in the selection process.

It appears self-evident that local priorities and needs, as limited by any local constraints (such as the all-important constraints of limitations on funding) are essential factors that have to be considered whenever selecting electronic resources. However, sometimes in the rush to meet patron and administration demands to become more electronic (and hence more "modern"), the fact that a vendor shows up on your doorstep with an attractive short-term deal on a particular product that holds forth the promise of getting the library out of a current jam can become an alluring alternative to a carefully considered program, and can thus often present a matter of paramount concern. Making decisions too quickly may staunch a wound, but a series of hasty decisions can and usually does lead to a feeling of utter chaos, not only for the library's staff but also for those library users who do not understand why the library's resources appear to lack coherence and consistency. It is thus extremely important for librarians with collection development responsibilities to monitor user needs and

"For all information's independence and extent, it is the people, in their communities, organizations, and institutions, who ultimately decide what it means and why it matters."
—John Seely Brown and Paul Duguid, *The Social Life of Information* (Boston: Harvard Business School, 2000)

priorities while negotiating the tricky and rapidly changing terrain of electronic vendors and products.

SELECTION CRITERIA

In considering selection of an electronic resource, the following questions should always be asked:

Is the resource authoritative?
Determining the accuracy of materials available through an electronic resource, and particularly those derived from Web resources, is critical to the selection and evaluation process. One of the strengths of the World Wide Web is the ease it provides for publication and distribution of information to the world. However, this strength is also its greatest weakness, since it essentially places the burden on the information user to determine and evaluate the source of the Web site's information (that is, to do the very thing that collection development policies have traditionally attempted to do for libraries and their patrons over the years).

Does the technology make the content of the electronic resource accessible in a manner that better serves users' needs than does an existing equivalent print resource that the library already maintains or could acquire, perhaps at a lower cost?
Some electronic products may actually be more difficult to use than their print counterparts, but others will offer significant improvements, particularly in the ways that a user can search for needed information.

Does the electronic resource fill current gaps in the print collection?
Electronic products should not be acquired simply because they are there and available or "neat" and "cool." Rather they should be added to provide needed resources to the library's collection.

Does the electronic resource duplicate information or material that is already owned by the library?
Due to the common practice of bundling of electronic resources, libraries may sometimes find themselves forced to

accept some duplication that would have never been contemplated or tolerated with print resources.

Will the library replace a current print resource with an electronic resource, and what are the pricing ramifications of doing so?
Some electronic resources do cost less, but only if the library also purchases the print version. Some publishers require the library to pay for the print version of an item in order to be eligible to subscribe to the electronic one. On the other hand, some electronic resources really do cost less than their print equivalents, and in the case of those that are frequently supplemented, such as tax or legal services and reporters, the savings in filing labor costs can be enormous. Some electronic resources are priced so that there is an additional cost (above the price for the current version or issue) for access to the archives of the resource. In addition to price, one should also consider whether the electronic resource contains everything that is in the print version. Are all articles included in the electronic version? Are advertisements and illustrations deleted? Is the electronic product as well indexed as the print version? Is there an index at all or is there exclusive reliance on word searches? And are any of these deletions in the electronic version important to your users?

If the electronic resource is licensed and not available for purchase (see Chapter 6), can the library continue to meet its current obligations to local or state consortia in regard to interlibrary loan or user access to materials if some materials are only available in restricted form?
Although it is unlikely that the boilerplate license will allow interlibrary loans, sometimes it is possible to negotiate terms that allow such activity.

Does the electronic resource require the purchase of additional computer hardware or software?
Will a new electronic resource run on your current operating platform? For cost considerations, the selector may have to ensure that the format of an electronic resource is compatible with existing library hardware and software, unless there are funds available for simultaneous purchases of hardware and software.

If an electronic product is selected, what format is the most appropriate to meet the library's needs?
For example, would a CD-ROM product or an online product best meet the needs of the library and its users?

Does your library have enough computer resources to handle the additional user traffic that this product would likely generate?
For small libraries, adding an electronic resource can create a significant problem: the library simply may not have enough computers (or suitable space for computers) for patrons to access the new resource in a reasonable amount of time. This problem is particularly difficult if the library must cease carrying a print version of an item in order to be able to purchase its electronic equivalent. For example, a large set of books, such as a multivolume encyclopedia, might be expected to be used by a number of patrons at the same time. However, if you only have one computer that can access this particular resource (or a number of electronic resources), only one person at a time will be able to access the encyclopedia.

Figure 2-1, "Selection Criteria Worksheet for Electronic Resources," on page 27 will also be a useful tool for selectors.

SELECTION DIFFERENCES FOR INTERNET RESOURCES

Although most of the selection criteria typically used for determining the appropriateness of print resources apply equally with respect to Internet resources, a number of important distinctions need to be kept in mind.

1. **The librarian is truly only selecting Internet materials, not collecting them.**
   Internet resources selected are not likely to be housed on the library's computer other than temporarily; the resources are merely accessed from the library's catalog or Web site.

2. **The librarian may choose to select items that in print form were never considered for purchase.**
For example, the library may have acquired only a few pamphlets in print form due to problems in cataloging, shelving, and the difficulties in making the items available. The equivalent publication on the Web obviously does not present the same handling problems for the library.

3. **Cost, in terms of purchase price for the item, at least, is not likely to be a factor, but the librarian must consider the overall cost of maintaining links to the resource.**
A resource that is constantly moving and requires, therefore, constant URL maintenance and updating, either in the catalog or on the library's Web site, may well be so frustrating as to be deemed not worth the effort, even if the information it provides is of good quality.

4. **Selection of Internet resources tends to take place at a sort of macro level, while most print decisions tend to be made at the micro level.**
That is to say, Internet resources are typically chosen in a more generalized manner than specific electronic resources. Selecting Internet resources, therefore, can quickly lead to duplication, and can result in users examining unneeded or inappropriate resources in order to get to the ones they actually need. It is also important to remember that by selecting a Web site, you are in effect selecting everything that is linked from that page, and not all of those links will necessarily be needed by your library's user community.

5. **On the other hand, while print resources are much more likely than online materials to be chosen without actual examination of the item but rather through reviews or approval plans, Internet resources will typically be chosen generally only after personal examination by the selector.**
However, a number of the traditional selection tools are beginning to include reviews of Web sites, so the practice of choosing Internet resources may tend to become, over time, more similar to the methods traditionally used for selecting print resources.

6. **Some of the library's Internet resources may be actually created or published by the library itself.**
   This circumstance is not often the case with regard to traditional print resources.

7. **Access is a critical issue.**
   If the server on which the resource resides is overtaxed and therefore slow to respond, or if it is often not available at all, the resource will probably not be selected by the library. Likewise, no matter how accurate and authoritative the information provided by the site may be, technical reliability problems can become a paramount concern if users encounter significant difficulties. An additional access issue to consider involves the number of users who may be provided with simultaneous access to a single item. A single-volume print document may typically be accessed by only one user at a time, but the same resource, when made available on the Web, can usually be accessed effectively by numerous, if not an unlimited number of, simultaneous users.

8. **Archiving and preservation issues are obviously much more problematic with Internet resources than for traditional print materials.**
   Quality Web sites come and go at the Web site owner's discretion (and sometimes whim), but a print resource, unless stolen, lost, or mutilated, will typically remain in the library's collection for a considerable time.

SELECTION TOOLS

In order to make good selection decisions regarding electronic materials, you will first need to "corral" a group of titles with review information using both a local and global information perspective. Therefore, it is important to determine a set of resources to be used to gather titles and then to apply selection criteria among various materials having a similar subject-matter focus. The selector will be looking for tools that can help answer the following types of questions:

- What is available? For an older title (and with electronic resources an "older" title may not be all that old), one

must also add inquiries into current availability. It existed once, and it was good, but is it still available?
- How much does it cost?
- Where can it be obtained?

A further consideration is quality, which must be judged both from a subject-matter and also a technical perspective:

- Does it deliver what is promised?
- Has it won any awards or been cited in bibliographies or reliable Webliographies?
- Is the vendor reliable? This assessment can be based on experience garnered through past purchases or upon recommendations of colleagues or reliable reviews.
- Is the resource authoritative? Electronic resources do not always benefit from the same formal filtering/vetting processes that have traditionally been in place with conventional print materials. Thus, authority becomes a primary selection criterion that the selector may have to consider. The selection tools you choose that are best are those that help you determine the authority of the resource.

Internet and other electronic resources can be identified and evaluated through the use of reviews provided through both print and electronic resources. Perhaps a little ironically, printed guides to Internet resources abound, and, of course, many Web sites contain links to pages with evaluations, though the usually anonymous nature of these "reviews" can make them suspect. Many print review sources (such as *Library Journal, School Library Journal, American Libraries*, and *Choice*) also include reviews of electronic products and services. *College and Research Libraries News* has included Webliographies for particular subject areas for several years.

REVIEW SOURCES FOR WEB SITES AND OTHER ELECTRONIC RESOURCES

- **C&RL NewsNet: Internet Reviews** *www.bowdoin.edu/~samato/IRA/*
  This is an archive, updated monthly, of the abridged online version of *C&RL News*. It contains reviews of Internet resources, written by librarians.

- **Current Cites** *http://sunsite.berkeley.edu/CurrentCites/*
  Current Cities is an electronic newsletter that contains use-

ful reviews of numerous electronic resources as well as print sources in various areas of information technology.

- **Educate Online** *www.educate.co.uk*
  Along with other resources, the Educate Online Web site contains a section titled "CD-ROM Reviews," which provides extensive reviews of CD-ROM products of all kinds. The reviews are arranged under broad subject areas as well as a "newest" category. Although the Web site has a school orientation, other libraries should find the reviews useful as well. The Web site also contains reviews of new Internet Web sites and projects, and includes annotations plus a software review section.

- **NewJour** *gort.ucsd.edu/newjour/NewJourWel.html*
  NewJour, an electronic discussion list, can help you identify new electronic journals. To subscribe, send an e-mail message to listproc@ccat.sas.upenn.edu with the message "subscribe NewJour" and your name. More information about the list is available at the Web site.

- **Scout Report** *www.scout.cs.wisc.edu/scout/report*
  Scout Report is a weekly electronic publication produced each Friday which provides reviews of valuable resources on the Web. Scout Report can be read from the Web site or from an electronic mailing list. Instructions for subscribing to the electronic mailing list are provided on the Web site.

GENERAL REVIEW SOURCES ONLINE

Following is just a sampling of the sources that are available on the Web to help in selection. Although the focus of these Web sites is on print sources, some popular electronic products are reviewed.

- **Amazon.com** *www.amazon.com*
  Amazon.com provides access from its Web site to various lists of "opt" or "best" books, videos, CD-ROMs, and other materials. The selector also has access to peer reviews and standard review media. Some selectors find peer reviews from readers to be helpful, feeling that peer reviews may be more in touch with the materials that their users are likely to want or like.

- **Barnes and Noble** *www.barnesandnoble.com*
  Barnes and Noble offers services similar to these at Amazon.com, including peer reviews of materials. This site has links to resellers of books with the ability to order with the Barnes and Noble Web site.

- **Bookwire** *www.bookwire.com*
  This Web site contains reviews and links to other review sources, such as the Boston Book Review and Hungry Mind Review.

- **Borders** *www.borders.com*
  The Web site of this fast-growing book chain is noteworthy for its reviews and links to the New York Times Book Review.

OTHER SELECTION MEANS

In addition to being reviewed in more or less traditional ways, whether in print publications or on the Web, electronic resources often lend themselves well to other means of evaluation, including:

- *Trial offers*—Vendors of electronic resources may allow you to mount or link to their materials without cost for a trial period. After the trial period, one must either purchase or license the materials in order to continue using them. Trials are often advertised through e-mail and library Web sites. Thus more users are likely to try the products and offer advice to the selector than is likely to be the case for traditional print materials. Some libraries (and publishers) limit trial offers to staff use, but others open them up to their entire user population so that feedback from users, along with usage statistics, can be utilized in the final selection decision process. You will want to make sure that the trial conditions are equivalent to the actual use conditions that would apply if you purchased or licensed the product and that you do not receive a poor demonstration version.
- *Demonstrations*—Vendors will often be willing to come to your library and demonstrate their electronic products to you. Again, be sure that the conditions of the demonstration are as close as possible to what they would be if the product were purchased or licensed. For example, you don't want to see a demonstration of a Web product at 8:00 A.M. on Monday when Web traffic would probably be much lower than on, say, Wednesday at 3:00 P.M.

- *Visits to other libraries*—Another way to gauge the usefulness of a product is to visit a similar library that already has the product and to see it in action there. This approach also provides the opportunity to talk with that library's staff about the product and their experience with it. To be really useful, the library that is visited should have a similar technological setup and user base as yours.

SELECTION TEAMS

Instead of relying on individual selectors for the final selection decision, many libraries are today utilizing a team approach for the selection of electronic resources, an approach similar in some ways to the methods that many public libraries have traditionally used for the selection of audiovisual materials. Such teams will often include members from both public services and technical services departments. Bringing together a team with both subject and technical expertise can be a very effective method for selection of any material that is expensive and requires equipment and/or software for use. A carefully chosen team of three to five members can be established with persons of differing expertise, and it can usually then manage both subject-matter considerations and technical matters, as well as gather patron and staff input as appropriate. This team could also be responsible for producing documentation and training sessions after the electronic resources are acquired. In addition, by establishing a planning and reviewing cycle with specified actions to occur at regular intervals, the team can go a long way toward helping to bring order to a potentially chaotic process. Because electronic products are still used in a rather unstable environment (that is, on the personal computer), embarking on an electronic acquisitions team approach requires team members to be open-minded and flexible. Change is constant and selectors must be able to make decisions in environments that are often more murky than crystal clear. Figure 2–1 sets forth useful selection criteria for electronic-resourses.

Figure 2-1: Selection Criteria Worksheet for Electronic Resources

Name of Product: _____

Publisher/Vendor: _____

Contact: _____

Phone/Fax/E-mail: _____

I.   Audience

    A.   Who will likely use the resource?

        [ ] General public   [ ] Researchers

        [ ] Students (K-12)   [ ] Library staff

        [ ] Students (College)   [ ] All of the above

    B.   Does this resource have broad appeal across all types of library users?

        [ ] Yes   [ ] No   [ ] Unknown

    C.   Will the resource require special training?

        [ ] Yes   [ ] No   If yes: [ ] Available at no cost from vendor

                                        [ ] Available for $_____

    D.   What type of user support is available?

        [ ] Unlimited support at no cost

        [ ] Unlimited support for _____ and then $_____

        [ ] Help Desk hours _____ Cost $_____

II. Content

    A.   What type and breadth is the resource?

        [ ] Fulltext   [ ] Abstracts

        [ ] Bibliographic citations [ ] Annotations

        [ ] Statistical   [ ] Graphics

        [ ] Other _____

Figure 2-1: Selection Criteria Worksheet for Electronic Resources (*Continued*)

B. What is the current size of the resource?

Number of records/items/titles _____

Megabytes _____   Number of CDs _____

C. What are the dates of coverage?

[ ] Retrospective back to _____

[ ] Current from _____ to _____

D. How will the information be updated?

[ ] Daily   [ ] Weekly   [ ] Monthly

[ ] Quarterly   [ ] Annually   [ ] Other _____

E. How unique is this resource to the library's current collection?

[ ] New resource

[ ] Equivalent of print resource already owned? Title? _____

[ ] Equivalent of another electronic product? Title? _____

F. Is there a need for archival access?

[ ] Yes   [ ] No   [ ] Unknown

G. Quality checks

[ ] Reviews   [ ] Demonstrations in-house

[ ] Free trial offer   [ ] Demonstrations in other library/vendor settings

III. Costs

A. Initial costs for the resource?

Setup/access cost $_____

Storage cost $_____

Maintenance cost $_____

Figure 2-1: Selection Criteria Worksheet for Electronic Resources (*Continued*)

    B.   Content/licensing costs?

        Flat rate/unlimited access $_____

        Flat rate for _____ simultaneous users $_____

        Flat rate per simultaneous user $_____

        Based on FTE users $_____

        Rate based on library holding of

        print resource $_____

        Other _____ $_____

IV. Access

    A.   Where does the resource reside?

        [ ] Vendor's server   [ ] Library's server   [ ] Web

        [ ] Other_____

    B.   What are the hardware and software requirements? If the resource requires special software, does it reside on the vendor's server or on the library's server or on individual workstations?

    C.   What is required to access the resource?

        [ ] IP secured address   [ ] Password secured   [ ] Other _____

        [ ] Proxy server   [ ] Bar code

    D.   Statistical reports are available?

        [ ] Annually   [ ] Quarterly   [ ] Monthly   [ ] By request

        [ ] Individual subscriber basis   [ ] Consortium or group level only (if applicable)

    E.   If this product is later canceled, will the library still have access to the information that was once licensed?

        [ ] Yes   [ ] No

Figure 2-1: Selection Criteria Worksheet for Electronic Resources (*Continued*)

F. Does the library have permission to locally archive the resource?

[ ] Yes   [ ] No

V. Licensing Arrangements

A. Can you download a copy from the electronic version?

[ ] Printed copy[ ] Electronic file copy

[ ] Both   [ ] Neither

B. Do you have the ability to make a copy for interlibrary loan purposes?

[ ] Yes   [ ] No

C. Are there restrictions on users?

[ ] Local, in-building access only

[ ] Remote access if authenticated

[ ] Walk-ins to the library may use

[ ] Must restrict to registered borrowers or faculty and staff or organization members

VI. Ease of Use and Appropriateness

How would you respond to the following statements about the product:

A. The search engine for this product is powerful.

[ ] Strongly agree   [ ] Agree   [ ] Disagree   [ ] Strongly disagree

B. The number of access points available is sufficient for most users.

[ ] Strongly agree   [ ] Agree   [ ] Disagree   [ ] Strongly disagree

C. Overall this product is easy to use.

[ ] Strongly agree   [ ] Agree   [ ] Disagree   [ ] Strongly disagree

D. If there is a print equivalent, this product faithfully reproduces the print original.

[ ] Strongly agree   [ ] Agree   [ ] Disagree   [ ] Strongly disagree

[ ] Not applicable

E. This product has the potential to be heavily used by patrons.

[ ] Strongly agree   [ ] Agree   [ ] Disagree   [ ] Strongly disagree

CONCLUSION

The selection of electronic resources continues to be a troubling proposition for many libraries. Selection in today's libraries covers the traditional factors plus a number of new technical and cost factors. The tendency of vendors to bundle or package a number of resources/titles/images has moved more of the selection process from a title-by-title selection approach to an aggregate approach. This new approach includes new decisions as to tolerable amount of duplication, consideration of differences in search engines, and analysis of differences in ease of use of the product, and other such factors. Nevertheless, the selection process remains important. Because of these various new technical issues, selection may best be accomplished through a team approach that incorporates members having both subject-matter and information technology expertise.

3 BUDGETING AND ACQUISITIONS

The work of a library's acquisitions staff is changing somewhat with the advent of electronic resources and the concomitant change in emphasis from direct ownership of materials to access to or licensing of those materials. Therefore, because many acquisitions functions are moving from a purchasing to a licensing environment, selectors must take into account copyright and contract law considerations. Another important issue that arises is determining what part of the library's budget can be used to purchase the electronic resources. And, if the material is to be purchased at the document-by-document level, should the patron or the library bear the cost for the article or item? In cases of substitution, does (or should) it matter whether the library previously owned the resources, but canceled the resource subscription or discarded the item in order to rely exclusively on document delivery services for the item? Consideration and resolution of these questions is a central issue in the acquisitions process for virtually any library today.

THE ACQUISITIONS PROCESS

"The economics of purchasing aggregated electronic resources in bulk, combined with competitive pressure in the library profession for institutions to be perceived as 'state of the art' repositories of cutting-edge technology has led many librarians to uncritically embrace these packages."
—Brian A. Quinn, "The Impact of Aggregator Packages on Collection Management," *Collection Management* v. 25, no. 3 (2001).

After the electronic product to be selected is initially identified, the standard acquisitions functions of verifying the bibliographic information of the product, identifying the pricing options applicable to it, and determining terms of its availability are matters that become equally challenging. A single database or electronic journal may be available from multiple sources, each with different search software, retrieval capabilities, and user functions. These choices, with their related purchase, lease, and subscription options, all naturally affect the price and availability of the product. To investigate these details, acquisitions librarians must work with vendors or distributors that specialize in electronic resources, or with their standard vendors who also offer electronic products in addition to their usual inventory. Of course, some electronic products may be purchased only directly from a particular publisher or distributor, as that particular company may not deal with aggregators.

Even placing the order for an electronic product may become something of a challenge, since the standard library ordering procedure may often need to be supplemented by a product-specific order form. In using such forms, the library is often asked to provide additional details about the anticipated use or number of users of the product, the equipment that will be used by the library, and the expected permanent location of the product. At this point, a license agreement may need to be signed before the purchase order will be accepted by the vendor. In the case of some vendors, the library may see the license agreement for a product only after the order is placed and the product has arrived, a process that may necessitate holding up use of the product until an agreement can be negotiated and signed.

PRICING MODELS FOR ELECTRONIC RESOURCES

For materials accessed remotely, most, but not all, scholarly electronic publications produced today require a subscription or license in order for the library's users to access the product. The way the pricing works varies somewhat from product to product. Following are a few of the more common models.

- If the library subscribes to the print version of the resource, the electronic version can be accessed at no additional charge.
- If the library subscribes to the print version, there may be a small additional charge for access to the electronic version. Publishers following this model, however, often require subscription to the print product before they will sell the library an additional subscription to the electronic version.
- Some publishers charge the full price if the library wishes to have both the print and electronic formats.
- Some electronic versions are available without subscription to the print version, at the same subscription cost as the print product.
- Some publishers offer an electronic-only subscription for slightly less than the print resource.
- Some publications are only available electronically, and they carry their own cost for subscription.

- Some publishers and aggregators operate on a "pure bundling" model, in which a library or consortium must license the entire list of their journals with no individual selections possible.
- Some aggregators of electronic journals and databases offer a pay-per-view option that allows users to enter either an established account number or a credit card number to access articles from journals that are not on subscription.
- Many electronic products are, of course, freely available on the Web.

BUDGETING FOR ELECTRONIC RESOURCES

The information resources budget of most libraries has historically been known as the acquisitions or materials budget, with the traditional purchases being, of course, principally print materials. As information typically provided by libraries expanded over the years to include nonprint materials, such as microforms and sound and video recordings, the cost of these materials was also included in the resources allocation schemes. In the 1980s, online searching costs began to be included in the typical library's information resources budget, and in the 1990s, leased information on CD-ROMs often became a part of that same budget.

Libraries generally do not receive additional or special-purpose funding for electronic resources, so that the costs of these resources are generally covered through the reallocation and redirection of existing funds. Following selection decisions, funding issues regarding electronic resources are next in importance. Libraries generally take one or a combination of the approaches outlined in the following.

- All purchases of electronic products and subscriptions are taken from the general materials budget of the library.
- Some electronic products or subscriptions are taken "off the top" of the budget before the materials budget is allocated.
- Some libraries set aside a certain percentage of the materials budget for electronic resources, or they may set up a spending ratio of books to serials to electronic resources in order to make allocations.

- Some libraries allow a portion of their materials budget to cover hardware costs or processing costs as well as software costs.
- Some libraries require purchases of electronic products through team selection or at least with a check-off system so that a wide-ranging review of a product is made before it is finally selected for purchase. This approach is also helpful regarding the broad range of subject matters that may be included in an electronic product, so that coordination across disciplines and between subject specialists and technical experts can be achieved.

The model that a library chooses to utilize is very important, because a growing percentage of the budgets of all types of libraries is now being used for electronic resources. This trend seems likely to continue and to become more evident in the near future.

CONSORTIUM PURCHASES

At one time in the not too distant past, library materials selection was generally an individual, that is to say, an item-by-item, process, with all steps in the acquisitions process clearly defined and usually pretty cut-and-dried. Most items were paid for individually, whether the item being acquired was a monograph, a serial, or an audiovisual selection. With electronic resources, there now exist a multitude of options for how materials may be acquired as well as a multitude of formats of the materials. The traditional primary skills of a selector (that is, subject knowledge and a knowledge of the publishing structure for the particular discipline involved) must now be augmented by knowledge of the technical aspects of the materials, consideration of copyright and licensing issues that may be implicated, as well as familiarity with various bundles of electronic materials (to compare coverage and prices). Ideally, selection must be conducted through a team approach and should ensure inclusion on the team of members possessing specialized knowledge in these various areas.

Since electronic resources are often much more expensive than print materials, many libraries are coming together for joint or group purchases of electronic products. Electronic products have really made joint purchases a serious proposition for many libraries. In the past, librarians talked a great deal about joint purchases, but such plans were all too often stymied when the question came up of where the material was to be housed. Each library naturally wanted purchases to stay on its own shelves, not on someone else's. But for electronic resources, group arrangements can avoid this problem and often result in a substantial savings for individual libraries while also adding a vital layer of coordination and expertise at a central level. Such an arrangement is, of course, particularly beneficial for smaller libraries that may not have the technical expertise in-house to do all the necessary technical evaluations prior to purchase. This type of arrangement does add a level of bureaucracy to the selection process but, depending on the library's size and budget, the additional administrative "cost" may be very worthwhile.

If a library is involved in multiple consortium arrangements, buying electronic resources in several different packaging formats can and usually will lead to undesirable duplication of titles and items. For libraries that are part of large municipal or state systems, funding bodies may, of course, be dictating these kinds of purchases through a centralized acquisition system or by requiring libraries to share resources maintained on centralized servers.

Library consortiums with paid training staff can help members plan for, acquire, and learn how to use and access systems and electronic databases. This network support may often be crucial for public and other libraries that do not have a centralized computing center to rely on. Consortiums can also spread such costs over a number of member libraries and thereby effect substantial savings. And since operational and maintenance costs should always be considered in the selection process, savings in these areas are important factors to be considered in the overall acquisitions process.

INFORMATION AT THE ARTICLE LEVEL

If document delivery is perceived to be part of the acquisitions process, then an important question to be asked is, "Who should control the requesting of articles from a document supplier?" Put another way, should document delivery be a mediated process with a librarian making the acquisition decision or should users be able to make direct requests from the supplier?

If the library already owns the document needed, then the library may find it appropriate to block or otherwise prevent the user from making an external request (that will cost the library more to obtain, for a second time) for the particular resource. If a document delivery service is used instead of an existing library resource, the service could also justifiably be viewed as a "luxury" service—for which the user should logically pay. Of course, the resource may not be readily available for a number of reasons (such as at the bindery or off the shelf), so in such situations should there not also be in place a procedure to handle service problems due to local conditions?

Recognizing this problem, some libraries use the blocking services of a document supplier to prevent users from requesting items already owned. However, many other libraries feel, even when document delivery costs are borne by the library, that potential user frustration (particularly where there are branch libraries or multiple campuses) outweighs the additional acquisition costs. Other libraries, doubtless for financial reasons, feel that users must foot the bill for document delivery services. It seems, however, that the position that users should pay for delivery must become less and less defensible as more and more libraries increasingly rely on online document services.

WEB TOOLS

A variety of information resources are available on the Web to assist the acquisitions functions. Some of these sample resources have information specifically about electronic resources and others function as electronic resources for acquisitions librarians.

BOOKSTORE NAMES AND ADDRESSES

- **Africa South of the Sahara: Bookdealers** *www-sul.stanford.edu/depts/ssrg/africa/afrbook.html*
  This online global directory contains an alphabetical list of bookstores with addresses. Telephone and fax numbers as well as e-mail addresses are also often provided.

BOOK AND OTHER MEDIA REVIEWS

- Booklist *www.ala.org/booklist/index.html*
  Electronic counterpart to the print magazine.

- **The BookWire Index: Review Sources** *www.bookwire.com/bookwire/otherbooks/Review-Sources.html*
  Provides links to numerous review sources on the Web.

Figure 3-1: Checklist and Budget Worksheet

How is access to an electronic resource best achieved?

I. Can the entire resource be owned outright or purchased by the library at a reasonable cost?

[ ] Yes   [ ] No   Estimated cost: $ _____

If yes, does the library presently have access to the hardware/software necessary for users to access the material?

[ ] Yes   [ ] No

If no, how much will access cost?

Estimated cost: $_____

II. Must the resource be licensed rather than purchased?

[ ] Yes   [ ] No

If yes, at what cost per year? (Please consult Chapter 7 for licensing $_____/ annually)

III. Would it be cost effective to purchase at the title or at the article level?

[ ] Title   [ ] Article

For example, rather than purchasing or leasing an electronic serial, would a document delivery supplier be able to meet the demand for the material at a lower price than purchasing/leasing the entire serial?

[ ] Yes   [ ] No

If so, what supplier is available? ### _____

Estimated cost of document delivery: $_____

Figure 3-1: Checklist and Budget Worksheet (*Continued*)

IV. Is the library a member of a consortium that makes group purchases?

[ ] Yes   [ ] No

Name of consortium: _____

If yes, consult with consortium management as to electronic products for which the consortium has made arrangements for group purchases.

Cost to library: $_____

If no, bring the product to the attention of consortium members for possible group purchases.

- Boston.com: Book Reviews *www.boston.com/ae/books/*

- The New York Times on the Web Book Reviews *www.nytimes.com/pages/books/index.htm* requires registration.

LISTS OF AWARD-WINNING BOOKS

- **American Fiction Prizes** *www.birdingonthe.net/litlists/ amfict.html* Lists winners of the Pulitzer Prize for Literature, National Book Critics Circle Award, National Book Award, Los Angeles Times Book Award, PEN/Faulkner Award back to 1970.

- **Caldecott Medal Home Page** *www.ala.org/ala/alsc/ awardsscholarships/literaryawds/caldecottmedal/ caldecottmedal.htm* List of winners of the Caldecott Medal for the best picture books since 1938.

- **The Christian Fiction Site** *homepages.ihug.co.nz/~dionelle/ books/goldmedallion.html* Lists of Gold Medallion Fiction winners since 1978 and the Christy Award winners since 2000.

- **Mystery Writers of America: Edgar Database** *www. mysterywriters.org/pages/awards/search.htm* A database of winners for this mystery genre award from 1946 to the present.

- **Newbery Medal Home Page** *www.ala.org/ala/alsc/ awardsscholarships/literaryawds/newberymedal/ newberymedal.htm* Newbery Medals winners for the best in children's literature since 1922.

BESTSELLER LISTS

- **Amazon.com Movers and Shakers** *www.amazon.com/ exec/obidos/tg/new-for-you/movers-and-shakers/-/books/ 002–4611007–9706421* The biggest sellers for the past 24 hours on Amazon.com.

- **Barnes and Nobles Top 100** *www.barnesandnoble.com/ bestsellers/top100.as*

- **New York Times Bestseller List** *www.nytimes.com/pages/books/bestseller/*

- *Publishers Weekly Bestseller Lists* *http://publishersweekly.reviewsnews.com/index.asp?layout=bestsellersMain*

SERIAL BACK ISSUE DEALERS' CATALOGS

- **Alfred Jaeger, Inc.** *www.ajaeger.com/*
  The Web site offers a limited number of this publisher's extensive inventory of more than 40,000 titles. You can also e-mail requests for items not found through the Web database.

STOCK AVAILABILITY AND PRICES

- **BookFinder.Com** *www.bookfinder.com*
  Special search engine that allows you to check availability and prices for new and used books at a variety of bookstores and booksellers. It returns a list of titles that match your search and provides you with the opportunity to order directly from the bookseller.

CURRENCY EXCHANGE RATES

- **Universal Currency Converter** *www.xe.net/ucc/*
  Publishers' Catalogs and General Information

- **Publishers' Catalogues Home Page** *www.lights.com/publisher/*
  Catalog directory can be searched geographically (city, state, country) by subject and alphabetically by publisher.

- **Directory of Publishers and Vendors** *acqweb.library.vanderbilt.edu/pubr.html*
  Alphabetical, geographic, and subject directory to various publishers' Web sites.

POSTAL INFORMATION

- **United States Postal Service** *www.usps.gov/*
  This site contains information about postage rates and fees, including international rates.

TELEPHONE INFORMATION

- **AmeriCom Area Decoder** *http://decoder.americom.com/* This Web site allows you to find the city if you have the area code or vice versa.

- **Telephone Directories on the Web** *www.infobel.com/teldir/teldir.asp?page=/eng/*

CONCLUSION

The process of budgeting for and acquiring electronic resources presents new challenges for acquisition librarians. The entire concept of an information resources budget often becomes murky regarding what can and cannot be paid from it. We as librarians have always worked on the principle that items paid for from the resource budget were owned and permanently retained by the library. Now we may be acquiring resources for a particular patron through document delivery; the document never "sees" the library shelves. The information resources budget may or may not include necessary equipment purchases for using the electronic resource. In addition, the new ways we can purchase or lease materials also bring challenges for the acquisitions librarian. Many of the new Web resources make many of the routine aspects of acquisitions work easier, but they do add another layer to the already complicated nature of materials acquisition.

4 ORGANIZATION AND ACCESS TO ELECTRONIC RESOURCES

by Ardis Hanson

The development of information infrastructures within libraries has undergone an astounding evolution of technologic advances. These infrastructure components encompass a variety of elements, including: the physical facilities to store, process, and transmit information; the hardware; the information itself; the applications and software that allow access, structure, and manipulation of information; and the network standards and transmission codes that facilitate interorganizational and cross-system communication. Clearly, in today's libraries, the largest expenditure of time, resources, and effort is in the management of electronic resources.

Management of electronic materials has likewise significantly evolved in a relatively brief time. Initially, libraries typically treated their few electronic resources as *rarae aves* ("rare birds"), with access easily handled by creating a separate Web page, overseen by a single paraprofessional or librarian. As these "birds" became less rare and proliferated into a vast flock, however, libraries had to adopt a different strategy, often by dividing collections into "virtual" libraries distinct from the "brick" libraries, and by diverting resources and labor into this new area. This strategy eventually proved confusing to the end users as well as to staff, who clamored for seamless access to all materials, resulting in the movement to integrate electronic resources with print materials.

The vastness of electronic resources now available poses new challenges, which requires that we rethink the approach taken in the 1990s. Today's needs focus on how best to inform and assist librarians in the acquisition process and to automate the upkeep of e-collections. Many questions arise, among them:

1. How do we manage expanding e-collections throughout a resource's life cycle, i.e., from evaluation, selection, and acquisition through renewal and cancellation?
2. How can we facilitate collection development decision-

ies to exercise more selectivity in the e-journals they license. The result may be a greater number of individual subscriptions with a larger number of publishers or more complex consortium relationships.

As collection budgets for electronic resources increase, it becomes critical to provide a locus for management information related to staff and patron needs. These database functions range from producing reports to managing acquisition workflows and end-user access, to public licensing display regarding terms of use.

There appear to be two emerging electronic collections management models, which may be described as locally developed (homegrown) solutions or commercial solutions. Both approaches have benefits for the library. The locally developed option offers complete customization and responsiveness to local requirements, while a partnership may feature lower long-term costs and provide a needed solution for consortiums or networked libraries. Added to these cost/benefit analyses are the human and financial resources required to develop either type of system, the problem of maintenance and training for multiple systems, and the establishment of new workflow processes.

2. **How can we facilitate collection-development decision-making and cost analysis for our individual institutions and our consortium agreements?**
Effectively facilitating collection development decision-making requires libraries to establish and review performance measures and to understand business processes (cost-benefit analyses). While selection teams, budgets, policies, and types of resources to be evaluated are important, the actual workflow and evaluation processes are equally critical. Establishing criteria, time lines, and consistency in reporting are preliminary steps to developing effective workflow.

There is a cost associated with the time and energy used by professional staff to evaluate, catalog, and maintain proprietary as well as "free" resources. Decision-making, however, does not stop with acquisition; it continues as collections are evaluated on a regular timetable to determine if the current configurations of electronic resources are meeting the needs of the institution. Critical issues to be considered include content, access, timeliness, cataloging, sustainability, usability, usage assessment and statistics, technical performance and service levels, added value, pricing structure, and licensing terms. A list of evaluative criteria and licensing considerations for electronic resources across eight domains was created by Pettijohn and Neville (see Selected Bibliography under Evaluation and Assessment): vendor viability, content access, aggregator databases, cataloging, archiving, usability, system access (network and copyright), and technical performance. Each domain has considerations for staff time, training, user impact, etc. For example, Pettijohn and Neville suggest that evaluative criteria for usability consider navigational tools, browser compatibility, performance on typical user or library systems, the quality of online help, search functions, and structural metadata. They suggest that licensing contracts consider usability and include a clause to ensure that the reliability of online connectivity should be comparable or superior to similar products, that malfunctions or defects be corrected in a reasonable time (also to be defined) and, if not corrected, that a library may opt to return product drop access early for prorated refund.

Libraries have developed a number of innovative solutions to handle cost-effectiveness decisions regarding the management of electronic collections. For example, the University of Kansas Libraries developed online subject fund reports that provide three fiscal years of subscription price information and calculate the percent spent from the serials allocation. Librarians can group title, financial, and publisher information by broad discipline as well as narrow subject fields, which allows easy identification of interdisciplinary titles across individual e-journals or as part of an aggregator database. The University of Nevada, Reno, developed a time-saving revised check-in procedure for its print journals and now uses staff time to establish and troubleshoot access to online journals. Owen Science and Engineering Library at Washington State University has instituted an evaluation of their scientific, technical, engineering, and medical journals to determine if special issues that are included in a journal subscription may help offset the decline in dollars for monographic collections.

Libraries and subscription agents can work together to simplify and expedite the management process. According to a 2003 white paper by Lugg and Fischer (see Selected Bibliography under electronic journals), existing relationships with subscription agents need immediate review in order to create new, more appropriate relationships with e-journal access management providers. Historically, librarians have used vendor services from cataloging and selection to workflow support and shelf preparation for print, and much the same services can apply in regard to electronic resources. However, today's libraries should define the services, data, and processes that they need to work both locally and through consortiums and thoroughly examine and evaluate the services vendors can offer.

3. **How can we best access prevailing license terms, such as printing permissions, remote access, and electronic classroom applications, such as Blackboard or WebCT?**
   There are numerous challenges in managing today's digital licensing environment. Increasingly, products require license agreements and often require extensive negotiation on the part of libraries. (See Chapter 6 for additional information on licensing). Licensing affects all aspects of library services and acquisitions. In addition to the plethora of business models, the fluidity of market, and new relationships and workflows, the problem of managing licensing is compounded by the fact that there appears to be no existing ILS or metadata scheme that incorporates licensing information truly successfully. However, it is important to remember that electronic journal management has many requirements and processes similar to traditional print serials management.

   The ideal electronic management system would track licensing and purchasing information about electronic resources, define relationships among aggregators, publishers, or vendors and the resources they provide, and selectively display information in the OPAC for public services staff and patrons. Further, the growth of electronic collections creates opportunities for standards, metadata, and data management.

   In short, libraries should have a list of working principles to guide electronic resources management. First, know the users: who are they, what data do they want or need to do their work? Second, know the uses. What information is necessary to know the "how" and "what" and "why" the collections are used? Be sure to factor in all your stakeholders. Third, be able to accommodate growth and, while growing the collection, design in considerable flexibility. Fourth, save the time of the library staff in developing a data management system. A data warehouse that can accommodate multiple views for multiple users based on the information they need avoids unnecessary duplication as well as multiple unlinked, stand-alone data sources. In building the data source, be sure to define metadata elements for all the users who are managing electronic collections. When moving to a data management plan, implement the plan in phases, at a measured pace so as to work out the bugs in software and workflow. Finally, incorporate usage data into the data management plan.

RESOURCE DISCOVERY AND ACCESS MANAGEMENT

4. **As we implement new applications, such as link servers like SFX, how can we manage electronic journals without duplication of effort?**
   Few tasks related to digital resource management are routine. Staff members report that, in addition to needing a broad and deep knowledge of the particular products they have purchased, they are faced with complex and interdependent tasks that require a broad knowledge of library systems, including networking and cataloging issues. From an administrative perspective, record creation and maintenance costs are often higher for e-resources, particularly e-journals. Many libraries create databases, lists, or title-level access to journal aggregators in their library catalogs. They also may use OpenURL-enabled technology to maintain and create access to library materials, regardless of format.

   Lists of electronic resources use the URL (uniform resource locater aka Web address) of the item they want to link to (the "target") from the item they want to link from (the "source"). This "hard linking" or "static linking" is very straightforward but a maintenance nightmare as e-journals continually migrate between publishers or as vendors change their URLs. Persistent Uniform Resource Locators (PURLs) were a step forward in managing resource location changes cooperatively among multiple libraries. A PURL is a URL that, instead of pointing directly to the location of an Internet resource, points to an intermediate resolution service, commonly referred to as an HTTP redirect. If a URL changes, only a single library would need to correct it in their PURL server and other libraries using that server would benefit. If there are multiple places in a

Web site or OPAC where a URL needs to be changed, the PURL resolution service would redirect these hard-linked URLS.

The OpenURL dramatically changes the manner in which resources are delivered to the end user. The OpenURL is a mechanism for transporting metadata describing a publication. The OpenURL syntax is comprised of a base URL and a query. The query is built of metadata. The metadata uses standard descriptors, ISSN, volume, author last name, collection name, etc., to create the query to describe the work and to deliver the requested item. This same metadata is derived from the descriptive cataloging and comprises the administrative elements for resource management. The metadata allows context-sensitive linking.

Unlike the "target-source" model, OpenURL uses a link server that determines to which target or targets the user should be delivered and the addresses (URLs) for those targets. The link server is maintained by the library, not the vendor, and contains the data in a single place on *all* the resources, print or electronic, that the library wants their users and staff to be able to link. Figure 4-1 shows an example of an open URL.

There are a variety of link servers (e.g., Ex Libris' "SFX," "Openly Jake," EBSCO's "LinkSource," University of North Carolina at Greensboro's "Journal Finder"). Link servers have different features, management options, and services. Link servers allow librarians to create menus of options (products and services) for the user. For example, when a user finds an interesting citation in an abstracting and indexing database, the citation would link to a menu

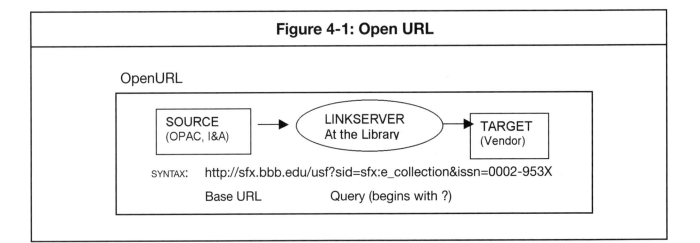

Figure 4-1: Open URL

OpenURL

SOURCE (OPAC, I&A) → LINKSERVER At the Library → TARGET (Vendor)

SYNTAX: http://sfx.bbb.edu/usf?sid=sfx:e_collection&issn=0002-953X

Base URL   Query (begins with ?)

of choices: the full text of the citation (journal or book), an OPAC record showing its location in print, a document delivery form, or a link to library service, such as Ask-A-Librarian. Figure 4-2 shows an example of different options a user might find within one citation.

A link server consists of a database and configuration files. In its database are: (1) descriptive information about the services, i.e., sources and targets that are available and can be linked to; (2) an activated link that turns on the title of each target (e.g., journals, catalogs, Web sites, etc.) that is available; and (3) decision-making rules on when a target will be "live." Decision-making rules basically allow the library to link only to those resources the library has the rights to access. For example, if the electronic subscription to journal X began in 1990 but the library only has access rights beginning in 2000, then the rule will not allow the patron to see the electronic holdings before 2000.

However, the use of descriptive metadata as a component of OpenURL syntax raises concerns about the accuracy and extensiveness of catalog records. There are a number of problems with e-resources that affect resource discovery. Errors in aggregators, such as missing issues, or lack of full text for an issue or an article, or incorrect bibliographic information affect resource discovery. In a recent study, errors were observed in 16 out of 28 journals (57 percent) studied by University College of the Fraser Valley (British Columbia).

Let's review the use of the ISSN, one of the most ubiqui-

Figure 4-2: Possible Link Server Menu

The American journal of psychiatry [0002-953X]

    Online full text provided via <u>Highwire Press</u>

    Availability: from 1997 volume 154 issue 1

<u>Search the Library Catalog for this item</u>

<u>Request the item via inter-library loan</u>

For publisher information, check

<u>Ulrich's Periodicals Directory</u>

<u>Need help</u>? Ask-A-Librarian or check our FAQ

tous pieces of metadata in the OpenURL syntax. The ISSN is assigned to every category of serial publications and is used by: libraries; subscription, microform, and bar coding agencies; distributors; abstracting and indexing services; and numerous others. For some of these users (such as subscription and bar coding agencies) identifying manifestations (print, reproduction, pdf, etc.) is critical; for others, identifying content (specific article from journal or subject) is desirable. When the International Standard Serial Number (ISSN) was created in the 1970s as an identifier of journal titles, electronic formats of serials as we know them today did not exist. With the choice between a single serial record vs. a multiple record approach for differing formats (manifestations of different expressions of a work), it is difficult to ensure that the user is actually linked to the correct title for the correct range of years to which the library has access.

There may be solutions to this problem. The ISSN Manual: Cataloguing Part (see Selected Bibliography under Organization and Access) recommends publishers provide all associated ISSNs of a serial on each version of the serial to provide comprehensive access. A MARC solution may consider additional elements in the primary ISSN field (022) of each version record since the current ISSN for other formats field (subfield x of field 776) is buried deep within the record and most libraries have not currently indexed them in their present catalogs. Finally, the development of an aggregator-neutral record may be a solution to reduce the current ambiguity of electronic resources cataloging; this presents challenges of its own.

Clearly the implementation of a new technology, such as Open URL, requires more than just adding a new tool to the library. To truly provide access and resource discovery to patrons, librarians in charge of electronic resource management will need the expertise of individuals in cataloging, acquisitions, systems, and collection development.

5. **How will new applications, like Metalib gateway, help us guide users to the best sources of electronic resources?**
New gateway services (or portals) are proliferating with the development of e-resource technologies. Gateway services can identify core content in subject areas through the use of federated, or cross-database, searching across a wide range of heterogeneous resources, such as catalogs, reference databases, citation databases, subject gateways, and

e-journals, that differ in the format of the information, the technologies used, and the types of materials contained in the resources. The user's query is broadcast to each resource, and results are returned to the user.

Gateway services also allow a library to create an environment of comprehensive facilities for accessing research, which can include locally created databases, projects for "one-stop shopping" sites, freely available digital content of classical publications, or access to electronic gray literature. Criteria to evaluate gateway services include: quality criteria and quality control; extent of metadata provided, and by whom; and the intended scope (subject, geographical, language).

Metalib (by Ex Libris) is an example of such a gateway. Metalib's strength is its KnowledgeBase, which is simply a collection of metadata about the resources that the library wishes to make available to its users. Each resource that the library wants to provide access to the user is cataloged in the KnowledgeBase. The descriptive information for each item includes holdings information, classification, subject heading and keyword assignation, and summary information.

Gateway services handle data discovery functions, while OpenURL applications, such as SFX, provide context-sensitive linking services that assist users in either obtaining the actual material or expanding upon the data already discovered. For instance, the linking services for an article might provide the article's full text or direct the user to the library's print holdings. Together, these types of applications may also provide information about the author (such as citation information or an e-mail address), the topic (such as relevant subject gateways on the Web), as well as the journal in which the article was published.

However, in managing these applications and services, librarians handling electronic resources need to understand the work involved in configuring the local database. There will be changes in workflow and additional staff input for the descriptive and administrative data in the back-end databases. For example, increased server traffic may place more demands on local networks and may expose other preexisting problems or connection failures. Other issues that need to be examined include accuracy in indexing of journal titles, consistency in the indexing of individual serials, identifying incomplete or missing information about the contents of the index, inaccurate metadata, and accuracy in licensing and access rights.

The working relationships between the library and its vendors will need to focus on developing win-win solutions for both parties. E-resources managers will also need to understand the limitations of the software, such as inaccurate bibliographic access. For example, vendor metadata often states that a journal title is full-text in an aggregated collection when only *one* journal article is actually available and full-text.

E-resource managers will also need to understand digital object identifiers (DOI) and CrossRef. An open standard, the DOI is an alphanumeric name that identifies digital content (book, chapter, or journal article), which is tagged to article metadata supplied by participating publishers. Paired with the object's URL in an updateable central directory, the DOI is used in place of the URL. The use of the DOI helps avoid broken links when an item's location changes. The DOI and the OpenURL work together. DOI directories are OpenURL-enabled. This means that the DOI directory can recognize a user with access to a local link resolver. Publishers of electronic content are increasingly using DOIs as the primary linking mechanism to full-text to ensure access to content.

The Publishers International Linking Association, Inc. (PILA), a nonprofit, independent organization comprised of a number of leading scholarly publishers, operates CrossRef, a system for the persistent identification of scholarly content and cross-publisher citation linking to the full-text and related resources using the DOI. CrossRef DOIs link to a publisher's response pages. These response pages may contain a full bibliographic citation and abstract, provide full-text access for authenticated users, offer pay-per-view access, journal table of contents and home page, and other resources. Link resolvers, such as SFX, can use the CrossRef system to retrieve the DOI, if the DOI is not already available from the source document. Unlike DOI and OpenURL, which are open standards, CrossRef is a collaborative membership network, and not a product for purchase.

When a user clicks on a DOI, the CrossRef system redirects that DOI back to the user's local resolver (such as SFX). It then uses the DOI as a key to the CrossRef database to access metadata that is needed to create the OpenURL targeting the local link resolver. As a result, the institutional user clicking on a DOI is directed to appropriate resources. By using the CrossRef DOI system to identify their content, publishers in effect make their products OpenURL aware.

NEW MODELS AND STANDARDS

6. **How will open architecture and support for industry standards, such as MARC, Unicode, XML, OpenURL, and SOAP, assist libraries in the management of their electronic resources?**

   With the proliferation of available electronic resources and growing patron preference for online access, it is natural that librarians, and particularly catalogers, take an active role in organizing and providing pathways to this kind of information. For many libraries, there is a more or less logical progression through these options and through various levels of organization. However, it is incumbent upon librarians to organize and describe them as fully as possible to accommodate diverse patron needs. Richer content representation, especially for prepublishing metadata and metadata for digital libraries, is critical to solving the problems of information discovery and retrieval of Web resources.

   Knowledge, to be useful, needs to be organized according to some sort of data structure or framework. According to the *American Heritage® Dictionary of the English Language* (2000, 4th edition), a framework is "a set of assumptions, concepts, values, and practices that constitutes a way of viewing reality." Data structures are developed to provide access to content. Content ranges from descriptive or bibliographic content to administrative content. A variety of frameworks are currently in use to describe electronic resources as a product or as a service, such as MARC, Dublin Core, EAD, Unicode, XML, OpenURL, and SOAP. The descriptive elements and/or content of an item in these frameworks comprise a "meta-vocabulary."

   MARC (MAchine Readable Cataloging) is a communications protocol developed in the 1960s by the Library of Congress for representing bibliographic records in a computer-readable form. In MARC, there are two components: the standard bibliographic description and a standard record format. The International Standard Bibliographic Description (ISBD) was developed to easily translate data across physical borders and machine environments. The

ISBD transcends international boundaries, allows records to be incorporated into catalogs of other countries, and finally, allows records to be converted into machine-readable form with a minimum of effort. The standard record format accepts data into predefined fields, is governed by a set of rules defining what information goes where, and last, but not least, is extensible.

Since this view of bibliographic data requires standards for data entry and configuration, the criteria allow for easy retrieval and precision and relevance in resource discovery and retrieval. This is a significant issue in knowledge organization and management, which can best be explained by the concept of "cognitive miserliness," the tendency of the human mind to expend the least effort in acquiring information. The term "cognitive miser" describes an individual's interest in conserving energy and reducing cognitive load, i.e., sifting through the mass of information that bombards us every day, ignoring anything unimportant to us, and retaining the information that is important.

The effective use of metadata, MARC, or any other knowledge organizational tool is typically based upon some form of Cutter's principles of organization. Cutter's Objects were to: (1) enable a person to find a book of which either the author, title, or subject is known; (2) show what the library has by a given author, on a given subject, or in a given kind of literature; and (3) assist in the choice of a book, as to its edition (bibliographically) or to its character (literary or topical) by providing numerous access points, including author-entry with necessary references; title-entry or title-reference; subject-entry, cross-references, and classed subject-table; form-entry; edition and imprint, with notes when necessary.

Cutter based his work on the principles of how individuals search for information, using his own experience. His experiences as set out in 1904 are echoed almost one hundred years later in the IFLA report on the functional requirements for the bibliographic record (FRBR) entity relationship model for works, expressions, manifestations, and items. However, one major difference between Cutter's experience and what is going on in the libraries of the twenty-first century is that today's technology offers multiple opportunities to share data (information) almost instantaneously across international borders in a variety of formats, queries, and formats.

Even though sharing data between catalogs is relatively

easy because of widespread support for the MARC format, translating content between different resource frameworks or metadata standards remains problematic. Migrating away from standard data elements with established descriptions to free-floating formats established by a variety of work groups results in a loss of reliability, redundancy, and the ability to replicate results. For example, MARC and Dublin Core records are not simply different structural representations of the same information. They also differ in granularity and meaning, some of which is lost when the metadata in a MARC record is converted to a Dublin Core representation. MARC, a national and international standard for over three decades, helps ensure predictability and cross-database searching. Predictability is ensured when Librarian A can be confident how Librarian B will use a particular field. Cross-database searching is facilitated through the use of authority records to create inter-record/database linkages. The Dublin Core (DC) record, by comparison, is very "creator" driven, and, as such, is only as good as the level of its creator. The person filling in the data fields in the record defines DC fields and also limits the level of complication. The DC's major advantage is that it is viewed as an embeddable element in an electronic resource. Three major disadvantages are: (1) the lack of predictability of a field, i.e., Field A may be defined "this way" by Librarian A and "that way" by Librarian B; (2) the lack of national and international standards; and (3) no current parallel system to facilitate cross-database searching.

The relationship between metadata standards is usually recorded as a table of equivalences, or "crosswalks," between corresponding fields, such as author, title, and publisher. These crosswalks translate between the different metadata element sets. However, the character data in the metadata element sets and the program files present another problem—translatability. Unicode is a standard for the storage and interchange of character data. It provides a unique number for every character, regardless of the platform, program, or language. It is a character encoding system, like ASCII, designed to help developers who want to create software applications that work in any language in the world. Think of Unicode as a way to internationalize programs, i.e., the code never needs modification since separate files contain the translatable information. The translatable strings are stored in resource files and are completely separate from the main code and contain only the translatable data. Variable (dates, times, numbers, currencies, etc.) formatting and processing (sorting, searching, etc.) are language-independent. Then, localizing that program involves no changes to the source code. A number of business programs and applications use Unicode, such as Microsoft Windows; AIX, Solaris, HP/UX, Sybase, Oracle, DB2, and MacOS. All the new web standards (HTML, XML, etc.) support or require Unicode. The latest versions of Netscape Navigator and Internet Explorer both support Unicode.

XML stands for eXtensible Markup Language (XML). XML provides a standard for defining containers that store information. This is extremely useful, because it simplifies the transfer of information from one system or program to another. Unlike HTML, which uses predefined tags to define attributes, XML allows the flexibility to establish new tags and attributes. Further, since XML is simply text, any application can understand it as long as the application understands the character encoding in use. The XML encoding of MARC data works at three different levels: record exchange (data transportation level), record validation (data conformity level), and sharing of services (application services level).

One of the first XML formats was the Encoded Archival Description (EAD) standard developed by the University of California-Berkeley for encoding archival materials and now maintained by the Library of Congress. The Library of Congress created an official specification for representing MARC data in an XML environment, MARC XML, which allows libraries to combine MARC data (e.g., the online catalog) with non-MARC resources (e.g., a locally maintained database or special collection).

The Open Archives Initiative (OAI) developed a protocol that makes it easy to send a query to a database over the Web and receive the results in XML, making it possible to perform searches of multiple databases simultaneously without the need for proprietary hooks into local databases. The Open Archives Initiative Protocol for Metadata Harvesting has been published with appendices documenting XML schemas for metadata representation (e.g., MARC21 records in an XML format, Dublin Core metadata format). Now that a standard has emerged for representing MARC, vendors and others will develop tools that take advantage of the huge amount of data already stored in the MARC format.

SOAP (Simple Object Access Protocol) defines the use of XML and HTTP to access services, objects, and servers in a platform-independent manner, bridging competing technologies and facilitating interoperability. SOAP consists of three parts: an envelope that defines a framework for describing what is in a message and how to process it, a set of encoding rules for expressing instances of application-defined data types, and a convention for representing remote procedure calls and responses.

The development and integration of these standards will radically change how libraries view, store, retrieve, and analyze information. However, from the resource discovery and management perspective, best cataloging practice includes the notion of specificity, the consideration of the user as the principal basis for subject-heading decisions, the practice of standardizing terminology, the use of cross-references to show preferred terms and hierarchical relationships, and solving the problem of the order of elements. Librarians can organize the information in such a way that allows the user to eliminate irrelevancies or false cognates and to focus on specifics, thereby reducing cognitive overload. Translated to the electronic environment, new models are being developed to support the management of e-resources.

7. **How will new models, such as the Digital Library Federation electronic resource management initiative (DLF ERMI) model, support librarians in the management of new e-resources?**
Although the literature indicates that cataloging remains critical to access, it is clear that descriptive metadata by itself is not enough to manage electronic resources effectively. Evaluative and managerial metadata is also necessary to provide more efficient support for selection, evaluation, tracking, administration, and troubleshooting.

The Electronic Resource Management Initiative (ERMI), a project sponsored by the Digital Library Federation (DLF), will develop common specifications and tools for managing the processes and workflow associated with collections of licensed electronic resources. The DLF ERMI deliverables include functional requirements, entity relationships, data structure, workflow, and research into the possible use of XML as a markup standard, any or all of which could be used for the creation of an electronic resource management (ERM) system.

ERMI is unique in that it uses a development partner model, i.e., libraries working in concert with a vendor or organization to develop product and standards as opposed to being a beta tester. Development partner libraries use drafts of the DLF documents to define their ERM system requirements. This innovative model partnership provides the library an opportunity to determine actually what it wants and needs the product to do at a stage when these requirements can more easily be incorporated into the product.

CONCLUSION

As we grow to think of collections by information content and not by format, resource discovery of and access to print and electronic collections becomes more powerful. Further, this paradigm shift in how we handle electronic resources creates new processes and services designed to support the service requirements of e-resources through complementing, rather than duplicating, existing systems deployed by libraries. New, and presently unknown, applications and work processes will have to be created in the coming years that will allow libraries a single point of administration for e-resources and a comprehensive solution for managing the complex and multidimensional relationships that characterize e-resources.

The use of HTTP as transport protocol; XML as a data exchange format language; SOAP as a message structure format; Web Services Description Language (WSDL); and Universal Description, Discovery and Integration (UDDI) and ebXML (e-commerce) as standards for directories of available services will permanently change the publishing industry. New and emerging standards will move libraries and publishing away from existing package—and product-centric models with the realization that the real value of their respective collections is in the ideas and content in those packages and products and their customers' use of that information. Contextual publishing is the next, logical step as these new technologies and standards allow the automated delivery of content into workflows and tasks in very specific contexts.

The semantic Web developments spearheaded by Tim Berners-Lee and the World Wide Web Consortium (W3C) illustrate the use of XML data representation to define customized tagging schemes for the representation of data. The next required element is a Web ontology language that can formally describe the semantics of classes in the many domains of interest and the semantics of properties (or attributes) used in Web documents.

Specialty Web search engines have emerged, including Google Scholar™, which searches specifically for scholarly literature on the Web, and Elsevier's Scirus™, which specifically searches for health, life, physical, and social sciences results on the Web. Yahoo!™ and Google™ have projects under way that allow searchers to search the OCLC WorldCat database as part of their basic search feature. These developments beg the question of how full should be the information on our library resources, both electronic and print, since users can now virtually browse our shelves. In addition, there were two recent project agreements to digitize millions of books that are in the public domain from prestigious academic and research library collections and make the books full-text searchable.

As we move into the next decade, librarians should contemplate confidently the opportunities provided in electronic collection management, especially in managing access to, and metadata about, e-resources, and they should participate actively in standards or systems development. Clearly, librarians have much to offer in the development of these new additional intelligent tools for integrated access across heterogeneous resources.

5 EVALUATION AND ASSESSMENT

Collection assessment can be defined as the systematic, organized process of describing the state of a library's resources and their effectiveness at a particular time. Assessment requires that the collection be measured, analyzed, and judged according to specific criteria for relevancy, size, quality, and use. Librarians have generally thought of library assessments in terms of their library's book or serials collections, but assessment and evaluation are equally important for electronic resources and in determining the effectiveness of a library's mix of electronic and printed resources.

In the context of this handbook, the focus is on assessment of the electronic resources held or accessed through a particular library and how these materials assist the library in developing a collection that adequately meets the needs of its users. If a library has an integrated collection development policy, and in most cases it should, then the assessment of electronic resources must not be conducted in isolation but rather in terms of how those resources fit into the library's overall collection.

If your library is operating under a separate collection development policy for electronic resources, an assessment can be configured solely to evaluate electronic resources. However, as stated in Chapter 1, the increasing array of electronic resources means that segregating them in policy/philosophy is probably detrimental to the overall planning and development of the library collection as a whole.

In addition to electronic resources that are physically housed in the library, most libraries now rely heavily on networked resources, which are generally accessed via the Web. Although some of the techniques that are normally used in accessing print collections still apply, networked resources do add complications to the assessment project. There are also some new techniques which can be added to the traditional mix.

ASSESSMENT DATA

In addition to statistics generally kept in libraries concerning the print collection's size and growth, libraries evaluating electronic collections will also need to collect data in the following areas:

- Type of Internet connection used by the library itself and that used by patrons to access the library remotely.
- Capabilities and distribution of computer workstations and printers provided in the library building.
- Internet and other network service costs, including the costs associated with remote dial-in capabilities.
- Web page and database hits, searches, printing and the like.

ASSESSMENT ACTIVITIES

Collection assessment and evaluation covers a number of different activities. First, the proper assessment of a collection involves a comprehensive description of the library's resources at a particular point in time. This description will include not only an assessment of past and current collecting strengths, but also an assessment of what the library's future collecting strengths should be. Increasingly, librarians must also look at the overlap in full-text resources among vendors as bundled resources often contain titles that are already owned or licensed by the library. An assessment project also evaluates the effectiveness of the library's collection in supporting the mission and goals of the organization of which it forms a part; it should lead to a plan of action detailing how the library's collection development activities should proceed in order to obtain the best match between the collection and the mission and goals of the library.

STANDARD AREAS OF DATA COLLECTION

Traditionally libraries have gathered qualitative and quantitative assessment data in the following areas:

- Circulation statistics
- Title count
- Median age of item
- Shelf observation by subject experts

- Holdings checked against standard lists/bibliographies
- Interlibrary loan requests
- User surveys
- Focus groups

The information gained from these methods is equally important in terms of electronic resources and how they fit into the library's overall collection. However, there are some additional data collection methods, set out in the following, that can be used to obtain, relatively easily, the additional information needed concerning the library's electronic resources.

Although vendors can supply statistics for the use of their networked resources, the proliferation of federated or metasearch software has led to a situation in which these statistics require additional study by the library to determine the true usefulness of particular sources to their patrons because of the very nature of the federated search. In addition, not all vendors report usage statistics in the same way, so care always has to be taken when comparing across vendor products. Figure 5-1 displays why evaluating networked resources can be a problem.

TECHNOLOGICAL ADDITIONS TO STANDARD DATA SOURCES

Scripted user surveys/assessments—Provides users of electronic resources with a pop-up (or some other method) box onscreen, allowing them to rate the value of the resource to their information need (a user survey, so to speak, at the point of actual use of an electronic resource).

Transaction log or Web log analysis—Provides data for analysis of user transaction activity at a Web site or in interaction with any electronic resource made available by the library. Some electronic resource vendors provide useful statistics about usage on a regular basis. These statistics can be used to make decisions concerning database renewal or the necessary number of simultaneous users. Examples of statistical data that might be gathered include number of queries per specific database, number of sessions, number of menu selections, number of items to examine, citations displayed, and the number of times users were denied access because the maximum number of simultaneous us-

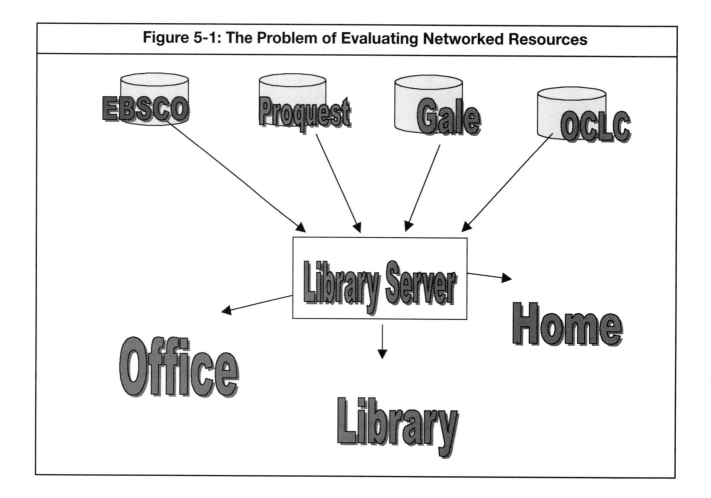

Figure 5-1: The Problem of Evaluating Networked Resources

ers was exceeded. Statistics, unfortunately, do not usually provide much information about the relative usefulness of a resource and whether the patron received exactly the information that was desired, but they can provide some information about how the particular product is being used; that information can then be supplemented through one or more of the qualitative assessment techniques.

Network usage analysis—Measures the use of Web-based services by collecting network or terminal use statistics, such as the load on the network server or router, user access points, and number of users. This information shows network load and capacity and indicates what services are being used and how frequently.

Vendor-supplied statistics—For networked electronic resources, the vendors can supply the library with a great deal of statistical information related to the use of the particular resource. Often these statistics are not comparable across products and almost certainly not comparable across vendors. Given that the statistics provided to libraries are nonstandardized, librarians must use caution if they are not to compare "apples and oranges" when making decisions based on those data. Vendors should be able to supply librarians with statistics in a form that the library specifies, but at the present that is not usually the case. It generally falls to libraries to attempt to keep their own statistics if they are to make purchasing and retention decisions based upon statistical data; however, most libraries do not have the staff to do a thorough job of keeping statistics across products and vendors.

The quantitative measures described in the preceding were initially the major ways by which librarians evaluated networked electronic resources, but as time goes by more and more use of a mix of techniques including quantitative but also qualitative measures (as described in the next section) are being utilized by librarians in their collection development decisions.

QUALITATIVE TECHNIQUES

Content analysis—The analysis of the content of a networked resource, including accuracy of information presented, aesthetics, readability, currency, and relevancy judgments. Although content analysis could also be performed on a print collection, this technique is much more likely to be used as a library collection assessment technique for electronic resources than for print resources. This technique is attractive because of the greater problems of authoritativeness that electronic resources typically present. Usability is also important to consider. Does the system "crash" when too many persons attempt to access it? Are the Web sites stable or do they move to other URLs frequently? Can you get "stuck" in the site with no clear way for the user to break out of it? Developing the answers to all of these questions requires devotion of significant time by librarians.

Focus groups—Small groups of users are selected to explore key issues in such areas as electronic content, performance, and services. One might consider focusing on both heavy users of electronic resources and also reluctant users to get a full picture of user concerns and needs. Do users find the library's electronic resources to be user-friendly? Can they easily find their way around Web-based resource sites? Do they find the instruction and help provided on online sites to be adequate?

Case studies—Particular "communities" of users, such as elementary school students, business-oriented users, researchers, etc., are selected in order to study in depth their use of your electronic resources and how electronic resources contribute to their needs and particular uses.

The preceding quantitative and qualitative measures can be used to describe essential characteristics about the library's collection, such as:

- Collection adequacy to support library services—Can the materials owned or accessed from the library supply the information needs of an appropriate percentage of library users? Each library must decide for itself, based on available staff and resources, what percentage makes sense for its particular situation.
- Formats and types of materials acquired—What kinds of materials are being acquired and, second, what kinds of materials should be acquired in order to meet the demands of local patrons?
- Usage patterns—Both in-house use and circulation should be considered. Do multiple patrons need simultaneous access? Do users need access from home or office?
- Language of materials acquired compared to circulation and ILL requests—Does the library need to provide popular and/or scholarly materials in Spanish, Chinese, or other languages?
- Reading levels acquired compared to items circulated— Does the reading level of materials acquired match the reading levels of the library's users.
- Current priorities compared to current usage and requests—For example, do the current priorities for materials as reflected in your budget match current patterns of usage as reflected in circulation statistics or in requests made to librarians and staff at circulation or reference desks? Does an analysis of interlibrary loan requests reveal an area of current demand, but few materials to support that demand are being acquired by the library?

Collection maintenance actions determined from collection assessments include:

- Addition decisions—In examining the data collected, which titles or groups of materials does the library need to acquire?
- Preservation and conservation decisions—Did data collection identify materials of local or heavy use that require preservation action?
- Replacement decisions—What lost or mutilated or heavily worn materials are still in demand by patrons?
- Updating decisions—Where has your collection become outdated and in need of replenishment with newer materials?
- Weeding decisions—Are there areas in the collection that are no longer being used? What materials have become too outdated to be of use to clients?

Some internal library factors play an important role in either the location of resources by patrons or in how the library operates. They need to be considered when planning an assessment project because they can affect both the data collection process and the interpretation of those data. These factors include:

- Cataloging and indexing of resources—Are the resources being evaluated, properly cataloged, and indexed so that clients can find the resources? Buying an electronic resource and not providing proper access mechanisms dooms it to underuse no matter how outstanding its quality.
- Screen display—Is it clear and are its instructions easily understood? Does it load quickly on the computer?
- Is the software flexible enough to accommodate users with disabilities?
- Is reading level separation adequate? This factor can be crucial, particularly in a public library setting.
- Circulation or use-counting procedures—Is the library accurately accounting for use? Are both in-house and remote use of materials being adequately measured?
- Collection management policy selection criteria—Has the library established adequate selection criteria, and are those criteria being followed?
- Purchasing and weeding data record-keeping procedures— Are proper procedures in place to evaluate a product correctly?
- Collection subunits—Especially in public libraries, the way resources are distributed among various subunits of the collection can be vital for the effective use of the resource. For example: Should it be available from the children's room? Near the popular fiction collection?

As new technologies and formats emerge, the nature of the library's collection changes. While the type of library will affect the mix of materials, Figure 5-2 shows a pattern that fits many libraries today. The traditional bipolar mix of print books and serials is quickly evolving into a triumvirate, with electronic resources becoming a major portion of many collections. This new category of materials adds a new layer to the evaluation process.

TIPS ON MANAGING AN EVALUATION PROJECT

The preceding pages have outlined a number of data items that could be collected in a number of ways. Obviously, no one as-

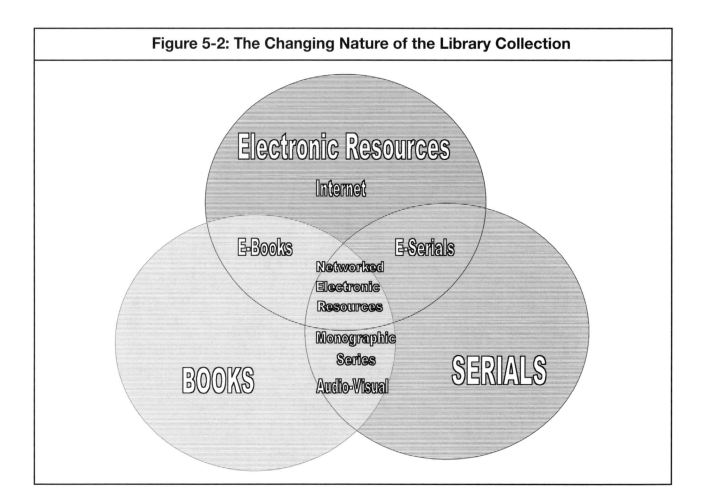

Figure 5-2: The Changing Nature of the Library Collection

sessment or evaluation project will use all of them, so it is necessary to consider first what you really want or need to learn as a result of an evaluation project. First you must have firm goals in mind for the project, know what audience or audiences it is intended for, and then determine what data are needed for the purpose/goals that you have stated. Simply collecting data for the purpose of collecting data will not result in useful information about your electronic resources. You may collect so much data that it is impossible to see the forest for the individual trees. So before you engage in data collection, carefully determine what is really required.

Once you have determined what information is needed, then consider how you will select the data. Data that can be objectively obtained from the report module of your online system, or from transaction log analyses, often will be more accurate than if you depend on users' perceptions of what they did. Such data are often easier to obtain and tabulate as well. However, a mix of qualitative and quantitative measures will give you a better feeling for the overall picture of your electronic resources and how they are accepted and used by patrons. Researchers generally agree that the use of more than one method gives a much more accurate picture of the "true" situation. Again, before collecting any data, think about how you will analyze the data. This step is very important in the planning stages, since you don't want to get to the end of the data collection phase and discover that you failed to collect a vital piece of data that you really need when you begin your analysis.

Now you are ready to collect your data. Be sure that everyone involved in data collection knows exactly what to collect and be sure that they do so consistently. Instructions and training of data collectors is critical to the success of any evaluation project. Once data is collected, turn the information over to the person/group who will actually conduct the data analysis. Then, when the objective portion of the analysis is complete, remember that interpretation is key. For example, is a particular electronic resource not being used because its content is not needed (a collection development problem), patrons do not know it exists (a marketing problem), patrons do not understand how to use it (a training problem), or patrons cannot obtain access to a workstation to use the product (a hardware availability problem)? This is an area where the use of one or more of the qualitative measures will help you make the correct interpretation. Users are the best persons to tell you why they are not using a resource, but the analysis of usage statistics will never give you that slant on the issue.

Last but not least, always write up your findings. In fact, you may wish to write more than one report based on the intended audience. In-house, you may want more detailed information to help staff make selection and policy decisions. Externally, by contrast, you may want to prepare a more general report that provides an overall view for board members, faculty, and patrons. Also, keep in mind that different constituencies may be interested in different data as they may have significantly different perspectives about library resources.

CONCLUSION

Remember that the evaluation of electronic resources is a new and growing area of interest in the library and information science field. While in the past we have attempted from time to time to evaluate various online services, the increasing array of electronic resources in libraries today is causing increased interest, but as yet there are no ineffably "tried and true" methods. It was inevitable that we would start out using data collection methods originally intended for print materials, and then gradually add more and more data to be collected that is strictly for electronic resources. This change will lead to more methodologies for data collection that are specifically geared toward electronic resources. The statistical data that is being supplied from vendors is often not standardized and can vary greatly among vendors. At present there is a real need for vendors to standardize the statistical data that is reported to libraries if librarians are to be able to make informed decisions when evaluating their networked electronic resources. Figure 5.3 shows a sample work form. We are learning more and more about doing such assessments all the time, so stay tuned!

Figure 5-3: Work Form for an Electronic Resources Evaluation Project

I.   What are our three main goals (external and internal) of the project?

    1. _____

    2. _____

    3. _____

II. Why are we conducting the project, i.e., who is our intended audience?

    1. _____

    2. _____

    3. _____

II.a. Who will conduct the project?

    [ ] Library Staff   [ ] Consultant   [ ] Library Staff with aid of a Consultant

III. Which method or methods of evaluation will be used?

    1. _____

    2. _____

    3. _____

    4. _____

IV. For each method, what data will be collected?

    Method 1: Data to be Collected

        1. _____

        2. _____

        3. _____

        4. _____

Figure 5-3: Work Form for an Electronic Resources Evaluation Project *(Continued)*

Method 2: Data to be Collected

1. _____

2. _____

3. _____

4. _____

Method 3: Data to be Collected

1. _____

2. _____

3. _____

4. _____

V. Will the library staff need training in data collection? [ ] Yes   [ ] No

If so, how and by whom will the training be provided?

1. _____

2. _____

Estimated Cost: $_____

VI. How will the data be analyzed?

Data from Method 1: _____

_____

_____

Data from Method 2: _____

_____

_____

Figure 5-3: Work Form for an Electronic Resources Evaluation Project *(Continued)*

       Data from Method 3: _____

       _____

       _____

VII.   How will the library use the information gained from the evaluation project?

       _____

       _____

       _____

VIII.   How will the library disseminate the results of the study?

       _____

       _____

       _____

IX.   What methods are in place to ensure the study will be utilized by appropriate decision-makers?

       _____

       _____

       _____

6 DIGITAL RIGHTS MANAGEMENT AND INTELLECTUAL PROPERTY

The rapid growth of online and electronic resources has had and is continuing to have a profound impact on our society, our economy, and our libraries, and has even begun affecting our laws and commercial relationships. In addition to the copyright issues obviously implicated through the use of the digital medium, the use of electronic resources is being increasingly restricted by the provisions of digital rights management systems (DRMs) incorporated into and made a part of licensing agreements required to be entered into by users of electronic resources as a condition to obtaining access. The development of increasingly powerful and sophisticated communications networks and associated information resources will continue to have a significant impact on intellectual property rights in the United States and around the world.

Copyright is a governmentally created right granted to the creators of literary works to protect their individual interest in their work through prohibiting the printing, publishing, importing, or selling of multiple copies of a work without the permission of the work's creator; in essence, it functions as a protection from unauthorized mass reproduction and commercial sale. As such, copyright laws can be viewed as a limitation or restriction on the unfettered dissemination of information. As a method for releasing the tension thus created by copyright laws, libraries have long been established to effect the dissemination of information on a mass basis, normally free of charge to the library patron, essentially through the purchase and maintenance of authorized copies of works

But with the development in the last third of the twentieth century of fast and cheap photocopying, and as the physical limitations on making copies otherwise began to evaporate, new problems arose for librarians. For instance, while there might be only a single copy made for any given patron, the aggregate number of potential copies was potentially extremely high. In fact, by the 1980s the volume of photocopying became so great that copyright holders felt that their rights were being significantly violated, and that the rules of copyright in the United States had to be, and they eventually were, adjusted to reflect the new realities.

Today, new forms of electronic resources have tremendously intensified the potential problems exponentially in this area, both for libraries and for copyright holders.

The basic philosophy underpinning copyright laws was articulated by the U.S. Supreme Court in a 1984 case:

> The monopoly privileges that Congress may authorize are neither unlimited nor primarily designed to provide a special private benefit. Rather, the limited grant is a means by which an important public purpose may be achieved. It is intended to motivate the creative activity of authors and inventors by the provision of a special reward, and to allow the public access to the products of their genius after the limited period of exclusive control has expired. (*Sony Corp. of America vs. Universal City Studios*, 464 U.S. 417 (1984))

Presently, under the Copyright Term Extension Act of 1998, which was enacted in part to bring United States law more into line with the tenets of the World Intellectual Property Organization (WIPO), copyright protection in the United States now extends for the life of the author plus 70 years. The 1998 law also provides that works with so-called corporate authorship, and works that are anonymous or pseudonymous, are protected for 95 years after date of first publication or 120 years after creation, whichever comes first. Prior to the passage of the Copyright Term Extension Act, works published in 1923 would have passed into the public domain at the end of 1998; these works will now remain out of the public domain until 2019. It should be noted that the copyright law also extends copyright protection to unpublished works as well as the published ones.

Under U.S. copyright laws, as well as the laws of most European countries, there are stated exceptions to the exclusive rights granted to copyright owners, and these exceptions are critical for libraries. In the United States these include:

- The right anyone possesses to use and reproduce materials in the public domain, for example, works created by U.S. federal government employees, works never copyrighted, or works that have passed beyond the copyright protection period.
- Fair use of copyrighted materials for the purpose of research, teaching, journalism, criticism, or even parody.
- Certain archival preservation rights for libraries, i.e., the

right to photograph, archive, or otherwise copy, in order to protect or preserve the work.
- Copying for interlibrary loan for the use of another library's patrons.

It is interesting to note that the German copyright law, unlike the U.S. law, explicitly states that the exceptions and limitations to copyright apply to both analog and digital copies, and makes no distinctions between the two technologies. The European Copyright Directive of 2001 (*europa.eu.int/smartapi/cgi/sga_doc? smartapi!celexapi!prod!CELEXnumdoc&lg=EN&numdoc= 32001L0029&model=guicheti*) also tries to protect exceptions to copyright at the point of use rather than at the stage of sanctions for circumvention, but it is not as specific as the German law.

Where to draw the line between creators' and users' rights has always presented lawmakers with a vexing and at the same time very complicated problem. Producers of works must be encouraged to risk creating something new while making their work available in some form to the public; if their work risks becoming free for the asking, authors may be encouraged to keep it a secret—the avoidance of which has always been a major justification for the copyright laws. However, users of materials also have needs, and they should enjoy certain rights that the copyright laws recognize. The proper balancing of these interests forms the basis for any discussion of the extent and nature of the copyright laws.

The Digital Millennium Copyright Act (DMCA), passed by Congress in 1998 in conjunction with the Copyright Term Extension Act, contains a number of new restrictions in regard to electronic resources. The U.S. copyright law now prohibits the "circumvention" of any effective "technological protection measure" used by a copyright holder to restrict access to the copyrighted materials. It also prohibits the manufacture of any device, or the offering of any service, primarily designed to defeat such a protection measure (for example, bypassing a password requirement or defeating a form of encryption). Thus, digital rights management systems (DRMs) are protected in the United States through the provision in the DMCA of legal remedies against such actions and against the suppliers of circumvention technologies. This anti-circumvention clause is one of the major legal concerns (and to a lesser extent by the European Union Directive on Copyright) that libraries have with DRM systems. In the United States, anti-circumvention appears to be an "absolute" offense, no matter for what reason committed; however in the European Union, the onus is placed on the rights holders to allow bona fide uses that are exceptions to the exclusive rights of the copyright holders. Thus the balance in Europe may fairly be said to be in favor of the user, not at the stage of sanctions for circumvention, but rather at the earlier stage of the very exercise of the exception constrained by a technical measure.

Upon the introduction on a widespread basis of the photocopying machine, many librarians had to become familiar with copyright law and its provisions regarding "hard" copies of works, and they now must become accustomed to dealing with copyright issues in connection with the electronic delivery of information services. It might be relatively easy to consider that the same restrictions should apply to electronic materials as those applicable to "hard" copies, except that the use of the former is most often restricted through licensing agreements, which are really extensions not of copyright law, but of contract law.

The Internet and the Web did not introduce libraries to the concept of resource licensing. OCLC, Dialog, and other online mainframe systems have for many years used network resource license agreements into which libraries have had to enter, but CD-ROM acquisitions, quickly followed by Internet/Web resources such as electronic journals and other full-text resources, have opened the proverbial Pandora's box of issues and problems for libraries in the area of copyright and licensing.

Many of the traditional fair use rights (or in a slightly more limited way, the "fair dealing" requirements in the U.K. and Canada and the exceptions to copyright applicable in the European Union) that libraries have enjoyed in respect of print materials are no longer necessarily assured in the new electronic age of information. As time goes on, contracts for the acquisition and utilization of electronic resources will become both increasingly more common, and at the same time more complex. This is an area where librarians generally have been slow to react. Although it is instantly recognized that electronic products do not "behave" in the same way as most traditional print resources, the corollary that electronic publishers will not want to, and usually will not, behave in the traditional way of print publishers is a concept that librarians have been slow to grasp. However, it remains an important requirement for library acceptance of DRMs that the systems must allow for "fair use" or "fair dealing" of protected content if the library is to continue to carry out its traditional role in making possible the dissemination of knowledge to all who trouble themselves to acquire it.

More and more, electronic vendors no longer offer to sell their electronic products outright. Rather, they simply provide to libraries something far short of ownership—a mere license of the right to use their products, and that license may be revocable in certain events. The significant contrast to a traditional permanent book acquisition, for instance, could not be more stark. Licensing and DRM systems have shifted the focus from reliance on copyright laws to determining what can and cannot be done with a work toward contracts between the rights holder and the user. Today, therefore, dealing with licensing agreements has become unavoidable for acquisitions librarians. Moreover, managing and negotiating licensing agreements has become a daunting task for many libraries as the number of available databases rapidly increases, and the variety of licensing restrictions and special clauses respectively applicable to them seem to be growing at an even more rapid rate. In addition, these electronic resources may also bring with them digital rights management systems that serve to enforce the license agreement.

PURCHASE VERSUS LICENSED RIGHT OF USE

When a library is acquiring any new electronic resources, a key issue to consider is whether the library will be actually purchasing the resource or only obtaining a right or license to use it. This distinction, which may sound inconsequential at first blush, is nevertheless extremely important regarding the fair use rights of the library purchaser, and regarding the library's long-term access to the material. From the beginning, the drafters of copyright laws have generally agreed that at least some kinds of copying should always be permitted. Over the years in the United States and in other countries, there developed the concept of "fair use," whereby a purchaser of, for example, a copyrighted book might lawfully copy without fee or restriction a few pages for personal use, copyright notwithstanding. The problem lies in defining what constitutes "fair" use, which is differently applied in different countries. (Most countries do not apply the "fair use" concept as liberally as has traditionally been the case in the United States.) The U.S. copyright law codifies the fair use doctrine in general terms, referring to such permissible purposes or uses as criticism, comment, news reporting, teaching, scholarship, or research. The law also specifies four criteria to be considered in determining whether a particular instance of copying or other reproduction is in fact fair:

- The purpose and character of the use, including whether the use is of a commercial nature or is for nonprofit educational purposes.
- The nature of the copyrighted work.
- The amount and substantiality of the portion used in relation to the copyrighted work as a whole.
- The effect of the use upon the potential market for or value to the owner of the copyrighted work.

Looking at these factors, and depending on the circumstances, fair use might cover not only making a single copy but also multiple copies. For example, the statute specifically states that multiple copying for classroom use may fall within the category of fair use copying.

The current U.S. copyright law also recognizes a "first sale doctrine," which allows the purchaser of a legally produced copy of a copyrighted work (for example, a book that has been purchased from the copyright holder, such as a publisher) the right to sell or loan that copy to others. But if the actual legal title to the work itself is still retained by the vendor (that is, if the work itself is not sold), the access to the work is said to be licensed, and the purchaser obtains only a right to the use of the item, rather than the full bundle of rights that a purchaser ordinarily obtains when he buys a book. This means that, since a sale has not occurred, copyright concepts such as fair use and first sale doctrine are simply not directly applicable.

These distinctions are important in the typical library context. For instance, a licensed right of use does not automatically allow the library to do all the things it typically and traditionally has done with its library materials (such as loan, circulate, or even sell the work to others). In a licensing regime, what the library can legally do with the resource being obtained is strictly limited to those activities or uses that are specifically set forth in the contract or license document pursuant to which the library acquires the item. Therefore, the license document itself becomes a much more critical instrument than a typical purchase order, and in the case of libraries, the terms of use contained in a license agreement become matters of such importance that they should always be carefully negotiated by the library with the vendor of the item whenever possible.

This distinction is particularly sharply drawn for library purchases of computer software. Many, but not all, purchase agreements for computer software now allow the buyer to make a backup copy of the software in case the original is destroyed. If this element is not contained in the purchasing agreement, Section 117 of the Copyright Act actually authorizes such a backup if the software was purchased, but Section 117 does not apply to licensed software. If a library is not a purchaser of software, the library has no Section 117 rights; rather, it has only the rights set out in the licensing agreement.

ASPECTS OF LICENSING RESOURCES

When dealing with electronic products in libraries today, licensing agreements are a critical fact of life. Initially, when many libraries began ordering computer software and CD-ROMs, the so-called "shrink-wrap" licenses printed in small type on the envelopes containing the software were often simply ignored; many users thought, probably with some justification, that these originally somewhat obscure and unusual (and often almost hidden) licenses were so one-sided as to be virtually unenforceable. However, most librarians have begun to realize that these provisions, as they have become more conventional in the commercial context, may indeed be enforced. Librarians also must deal with licenses for Web-accessed databases and journals, where they must sign a license agreement with a publisher or distributor before being able to access the resource at all. With this in mind, it is always advisable to inquire about the terms of the applicable licensing agreement before ordering a product. Many publishers are quite willing to send the library an advance copy of the license agreement; the library can thus review the license to determine whether the intended use is indeed allowed. Some publishers, unfortunately, do not even mention the existence of a licensing agreement in their catalogs and brochures, and the contract is simply sent after the order is placed. It thus remains possible for a product to be received and the invoice in respect of it paid before the library even gets the contract and sees the conditions imposed on its usage of the product—a most unhappy situation.

Librarians entering into licensing agreements face four major challenges:

- Understanding the content.
- Determining the wording required for their institution.
- Pinpointing those areas of the contract that require negotiation.
- Identifying who should negotiate and sign the agreement.

When licensing content from an international publisher, it is also important for the library to consider that there exist treaties binding not only those in the country in which it is located, but also the level of copyright protection provided by the laws of the country where the publisher resides or is headquartered.

CONSIDERATIONS IN LICENSE NEGOTIATION

The rights the library may have to search, copy, and use the information contained in a licensed resource are strictly those set forth in the license agreement. Librarians today typically face one of two basic licensing concepts:

- Contracts for online services or access licenses (for example, Lexis-Nexis), usually manifested by a specific written contract signed by at least the licensee.
- Contracts governing the use of a licensor's software on the licensee's equipment or network (that is, software licenses). Agreement of the parties to the terms of such a contract usually is not evidenced by a signed contract at all but rather by a broken shrink-wrap package or a click-through "OK" initiated by the licensee installing the software, without which click the software cannot be installed.

Access licenses involve significant ongoing obligations not typically or necessarily involved with software licenses, such as the licensor's obligations to provide access or the licensee's continuing obligation to pay for services as received. Software licenses are not always viewed by librarians as being distinct from the ownership of the works involved, but this distinction is important because they are not the same. With a license, the right to use the information is typically all you get. Complicating matters, license agreements used by different vendors vary widely and are neither standardized nor all that predictable, so it is important to read each license carefully and consider the following points:

- How does the vendor define "site" and "user"? For example, a site could be undesirably limited to a particular computer, a particular building, or a particular campus.

A user could be a registered borrower for a public library, a faculty or staff member or a student for an academic library or school media center, an onsite user, anyone who comes into the library, or anyone who accesses the library via the Internet.

- Can off-site users obtain access to the electronic resource?
- If a library has multiple branches or has units or access nodes located on several campuses, does the license cover only the main branch/campus or are all of the locations appropriately provided for?
- Can users print, download, or copy from the resource? If so, is there a limit to the number of copies? Some licenses may specify the number of copies, and, if so, the library will be responsible for communicating these restrictions to its users.
- Is the library allowed to make copies of the electronic resource, or portions thereof, for interlibrary loan purposes?
- Will you have permanent rights to the information that is licensed in case a licensed database is subsequently canceled or removed by the publisher? Do you have the right to archive the material?
- Does the vendor's software contain electronic "self-help" or a "time bomb" or similar provision which, after a certain period of time, allows the vendor unilaterally to shut down the library's use of an application or resource, either remotely by the vendor or automatically?
- Are you licensing material that is already in the public domain? Oftentimes expensive bundles of electronic resources include public domain material as a large portion of the licensed product.
- Does the license limit your ability to enhance the information, so long as content integrity is maintained, to make the resource more easily usable by the library's patrons (such as by adding annotations or links to other holdings)?
- What happens if there are unauthorized uses of the resource? A license agreement should not hold the licensee liable for unauthorized uses so long as the licensee has implemented reasonable and appropriate measures to notify its users of restrictions. If such uses occur, the licensor should be required to give the licensee notice of any suspected license violations and allow a reasonable time for the licensee to look into the matter and take corrective actions if appropriate.
- Does the license agreement hold the licensee harmless from any actions based on a claim that use of the resource in

accordance with the license infringes any patent, copyright, or trademark or trade secret of any third party?
- How may you terminate the license? The contract should provide termination rights that are appropriate for each party.

Most importantly, the person reviewing the proposed license for the library should never assume anything. Always make sure that everything that the library needs is indeed covered in the license.

CHOOSING A LICENSE NEGOTIATOR

Unfortunately, the acquisition of electronic products means that someone in the library needs to be prepared to negotiate or conduct preliminary negotiations with the licensor/vendors. The following is a list of possible choices for the role of negotiator:

- Library Director
- Assistant Director
- Acquisitions Librarian
- Systems Librarian
- Counsel for the Library/University/Business

Some libraries use a team approach, or combination of people, and do not designate a single individual as the person responsible for all license negotiations. Often a designated individual from the library will work with the vendor to negotiate needed language and then refer the contract to the organization's attorney for final wording and approval. In any event, it is important for everyone involved to learn the "legalese" of licensing and know what the required language may be for your library or institution. The library should also develop and follow baseline standards for what is acceptable for its licensing contracts. The librarian or other person designated for preliminary license negotiations should be prepared to reject offers and terminate negotiations if no reasonable solution is possible. Products that do not offer licensing contracts that can be made satisfactory for a particular library's clientele may simply not be worth the cost of the license. After all, what good is an electronic resource if you cannot effectively use it?

It is best not to abdicate responsibility to legal counsel for deciding whether to sign a particular license. The attorney will understand the legal ramifications and be able to explain them to you, but the attorney will not necessarily understand the ramifications of the license restrictions from a library user point of view. Librarians must stay involved in the process to ensure that licenses for electronic materials contain only those provisions that the library and its users can live with.

In general, it appears that licensing agreements are of late becoming a bit more favorable for library users—as librarians become more familiar with and adept at negotiating, and as publishers and vendors become more familiar with typical library needs and more comfortable with removing or modifying restrictions in their agreements to accommodate those needs. It appears that, at first, either the library market was deemed not to be the major market for particular electronic products, or vendors simply did not conceive of how to write a license for the library market. These initial problems are fortunately fast becoming obsolete with more and more electronic resource vendors catering to the library market.

LICENSING CONSIDERATIONS

All rights and permissions need to be completely described in a document provided by each publisher or vendor for each electronic product. Some publishers require subscribers to officially and formally sign a license. In such a case, it is necessary to ensure that someone who has the authority to commit the organization to a contract is the individual who signs the contract. Few organizations will allow a collection development librarian or an acquisitions librarian to sign an official contract. Other publishers simply provide a document that describes the conditions and terms governing the use of the resource. Figure 6-1 shows a sample work form. Although electronic aggregators cannot sign contracts on your behalf, many will collect them and provide them for your review. They can also frequently assist you if it is necessary to negotiate terms in order to satisfy the requirements of your institution or governmental agency. It is vitally important for you to read and understand the requirements for each product, even when the agreement is a "shrink-wrap" or "click-through" license on a product downloaded from the Web.

Figure 6-1: Licensing and Negotiation Work Form

I.   Who will be responsible for negotiating the license?

_____

II.   How does the proposed license define both the "site" and an "authorized user"?

Site: _____

_____

Authorized User: _____

_____

III.   How does the library determine who its "authorized users" will be?

_____

_____

IV.   May off-site users obtain access to the electronic resource?

                [ ] Yes   [ ] No

Under what conditions or restriction?

_____

_____

_____

V.   Does the license allow users to   print? ____ Limitations: ____

                                                 download? ____ Limitations: _____

                                                 copy? ____ Limitations: _____

Can the library make a copy for ILL purposes? ___ Limitations_____

Figure 6-1: Licensing and Negotiation Work Form (*Continued*)

VI.   Will the library have permanent access to the information if the license is subsequently cancelled or the resource removed by the publisher?

[ ] Yes   [ ] No

What alternatives are available for access? _____

_____

Is there a commitment from the vendor to archive?

[ ] Yes   [ ] No

If yes, what are the vendor's access policies? _____

_____

May the library archive the material

[ ] Yes   [ ] No

If yes, what restrictions apply? _____

_____

VII. Are you proposing to license material that is already in the public domain?

[ ] Yes   [ ] No

If so, where? _____

_____

VIII. What happens under the license if there are unauthorized uses made of the resource?

_____

_____

_____

IX.   Does the license agreement hold you the licensee harmless from any actions based on a claim that use of the resource in accordance with the license infringes any patent, copyright, trademark, or trade secrets of any third party?

[ ] Yes   [ ] No

Figure 6-1: Licensing and Negotiation Work Form (*Continued*)

X.   How may you terminate the license?

_____

_____

XI.   How may the licensor terminate the license?

_____

_____

BEST PRACTICES

A number of organizations have put together useful standards for licensing agreements. These standards include:

- **Association of Research Libraries**
  "Licensing Electronic Resources: Strategic and Practical Considerations for Signing Electronic Information Delivery Agreements." *http://arl.cni.org/scomm/licensing/licbooklet.html*
  Contains major considerations and good approaches to licensing electronic resources.

- **Columbia University Libraries**
  "Electronic Resource Coordinator Draft License Agreement Checklist." *www.columbia.edu/cu/libraries/inside/ner/license-checklist.html*
  Contains a checklist of 17 items that cover some of the most important rights and provisions to look for in a licensing agreement.

- **European Bureau of Library, Information and Documentation Associations**
  "EBLIDA Position Papers and Statements: Intellectual Property Rights."
  www.eblida.org/

Although the site is focused on European law, there are helpful links and information on licensing in general, including consortia.

- **Licensing Models Web Site**
  "Model standard licenses for use by publishers, librarians and subscription agents for electronic resources" *www.licensingmodels.com*
  Standard licenses designed for the acquisition of electronic journals and other electronic resources. Four separate licenses are provided in various formats for single academic institutions, academic consortiums, public libraries, and corporate and other special libraries. Commentary is provided for each of the four licenses.

- **New England Law Library Consortium**
  "NELLCO Decision Criteria Worksheet for Electronic Acquisitions." *www.nellco.org/general/criteria.htm*
  Sets out a 31-question checklist geared toward law libraries, but the ideas and concepts behind the questions can easily be used and adapted by other types of libraries. This checklist covers much more than simply licensing issues.

- **University of Texas System**
  "Software and Database License Agreement Checklist." *www.utsystem.edu/OGC/intellectualproperty/dbckfrm1.htm*
  Covers eight major areas of concern, and guides librarians through a typical analysis of a licensing contract.

- **Yale University**
  "Licensing Digital Information: A Resource for Librarians." *www.library.yale.edu/~llicense/index.shtml*
  Presents a collection of materials with the purpose of providing librarians with a better understanding of the issues raised by licensing agreements in the digital age.

DIGITAL RIGHTS MANAGEMENT (DRM)

Digital rights management is a technological area that remains very much in its infancy; a multitude of issues still need to be resolved. As librarians, we tend to focus on the problems for libraries, but to be fair it should be noted that fair digital rights management is currently a source of confusion and complexity for the publishers as well.

What exactly constitutes digital rights management? DRM includes a range of technologies that give rights owners varying degrees of control over how digital content and services may be used. Generally, DRM technologies enable copyright holders to protect their electronically accessible material from unauthorized use through either software and/or hardware, and to determine under what circumstances users can access the digital content. DRM inherently deals with contracts—a license is a form of a contract. Beyond controlling simple access to digital materials, it can also control specific operations on the content, such as the ability to print, copy, or save, and it can also limit the number of times a particular operation can be done, such as allowing a document to be viewed for a maximum of, say, four times. Most DRM systems persistently protect materials, meaning that the content is never in an unencrypted state during storage, distribution, or use. (See Figure 6–2 for a diagram of a sample DRM system.) In order for end-users to access DRM-controlled material, they must have a key, permit, or license before receiving the content.

DRM is usually associated with the management and protection of publishers' assets from e-books, e-serials, e-music, electronic databases, and compressed and/or digital films or videos. However, it should be remembered that DRM technologies may also be utilized by companies or organizations that need to protect their internal documents from unauthorized users.

DRM can be viewed as a new business model that utilizes the almost unlimited potential of the Web, or it can be viewed as a restriction on fair use and even upon free speech. Some DRM opponents go so far as to state that the acronym really stands for "Digital Restriction Management." Although DRM systems are usually viewed as enforcing or protecting copyrights, DRM can easily go beyond protecting copyrights, since it is just as easy for a DRM system to prevent access to a public domain work as to one protected by copyright. DRM can also be used to compel users to view materials such as commercials (or an FBI warning on a DVD) that they might wish to avoid. Whether you view DRM as a "good" or "evil" technology depends greatly upon your position as either a user or producer of digital information and on the particular implementation of DRM technologies.

DRM technologies impose controls on content that correspond to contractual or license terms, regardless of whether or not these license terms conform to copyright law provisions regarding fair use. A library can enter into a contract that limits rights formerly guaranteed under copyright law [U.S. Code. Title 17, Section 108 (f)(4)]. Unlike the situation with traditional print publications, there is no going beyond what the vendor sets as the restrictions for use without further negotiations with the licensor. In the past, libraries have relied heavily on the fair use aspects of the copyright laws that allow for liberal use of copyrighted materials for educational use, research, and personal use in order to permit the library to deliver services to their users. Fair use activities do not require the authorization of the rights holder, so libraries did not need to seek permission for such use. Libraries must ensure that that any DRM systems that control the use of licensed materials do not eliminate the public, educational, and library user rights that the copyright laws allow.

Privacy and the protection of data are also issues to be considered with DRM. DRM systems by their very nature allow the tracking of usage by individual users. Within the European Union such tracking is lawful as long as the user is informed and gives informed consent to the tracking. In the United States, many libraries are operating under state-mandated privacy laws that may forbid such tracking. At their simplest, DRM systems impose restrictions on what individuals can do with materials that are bought or licensed from a vendor or rights holder. At the next level of control, DRM systems can report back to the vendor or rights holder on the activities of users. Such reporting could be part of a pay-per-view system, or it could report back to the rights holder all attempts to make unauthorized copies or unauthorized use. Often there are third parties, who monitor and collect information about the use of the items. This activity is usually not well disclosed, since knowledge of these data-collecting activities requires reading the fine print in privacy statements.

DRM technologies can be used in a variety of business models for distribution of content including paid downloads, subscriptions, pay-per-view (or pay-per-listen), usage metering, peer-to-peer distribution, and selling rights. It is important for librarians to be alert to the proper balance between DRM uses and user rights as the technology is still developing.

DRM SYSTEMS

Currently there are a number of DRM architectural approaches that allow copyright holders to control the use of their copyrighted works. These systems may make use of a number of forms of proprietary rendering software such as Adobe Acrobat (PDF) or all or part of the RealNetworks Media Suite or the Content Scrambling System (CSS) for DVDs or many others. There is no one system that predominates in the marketplace at this point as the technology is still evolving, but it is important to note that, at present, interoperability between these different technologies is almost nil, a situation that has serious implications for libraries and individual consumers. Whatever approach is used, DRM systems associate rules to content that are generally used to impose constraints on the use and distribution of electronic materials. The DRM system thereby serves to enforce the license between a content provider and the consumer.

The basic functions of a DRM system are:

- controlling the access to copyrighted works and possibly other information products;
- restricting the unauthorized copying of those works;
- identifying the relevant copyright holders and possibly the conditions of use; and
- protecting the integrity of the identification information.

In short, DRM includes everything that someone does with content in order to trade or make use of it.

The components of a DRM system can include all or some of the following:

- secure containers which make the content inaccessible to nonauthorized users;
- rights expression which describes to whom the content is authorized for use;
- content identification and description system to identify content and to associate descriptive metadata with it;
- identification of people and organizations that are intended to interact with the content;
- algorithms to authenticate people or organizations that desire to interact with the content;
- technologies to persistently associate the identifiers and other information with the content (watermarks, fingerprints, etc.);

- mechanisms to report events such as the purchase of a piece of content (pay-per-view); and
- payment systems.

Some or all of these components work together to provide a trusted environment for the secure handling of digital content between the contracting or licensing parties.

The process of using a document from a DRM-controlled source involves:

- user request for a resource from a remote source through a file transfer or through streaming technologies;
- encryption of files in an individualized form for the user's environment;
- user attempts to take some action (such as making a copy) and the rendering application determines whether the request requires authorization;
- if necessary, the attributes of the user's request is sent to a license server by a DRM client component;
- license server determines the applicable policies or rules based on the submitted request attributes;
- if the use is not already licensed, a financial transaction may occur;
- a license package is assembled and securely transferred to the client;
- DRM client authenticates the received policies/rules, decrypts the content, and issues an authorization for viewing or printing or whatever action was requested; and only then
- content is rendered or otherwise used as requested by the end-user.

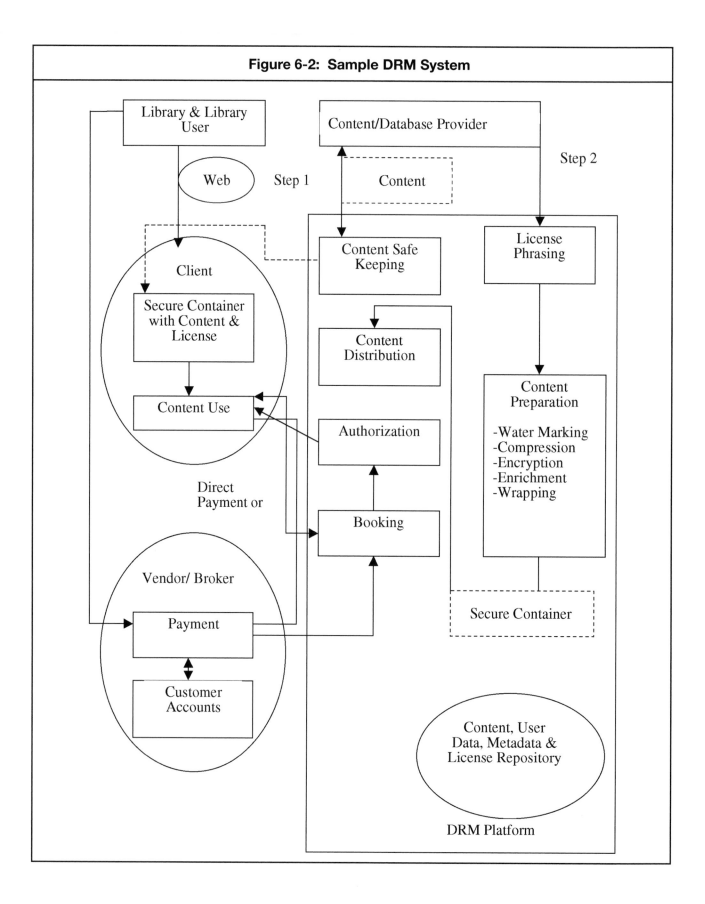

Figure 6-2: Sample DRM System

Authorization is the process of determining whether or not the requested use of information/content is allowed under the licensing agreement.

Clients are the components of the DRM system that reside on the library's side, such as the rendering application and the user's identification mechanism.

Encryption is the use of algorithms that restrict access, analysis, and manipulation of digital materials in their native form without proper access authorization.

Licensing phrasing is the process of determining the conditions under which the content providers offer their materials. These conditions may be standardized or be defined individually for each client or group of users.

Watermarking involves embedding a signal directly into the content; an example of one type of DRM system is provided in the diagram in Figure 6-2. DRM systems may be more simplified than this one, but most of the potential attributes of a DRM system are represented in the diagram. The signal is imperceptible to humans but can be detected by a computer. The signal represents the license associated with the content. In addition to watermarking, copyright holders can also create digital identifiers for copies of their works by "fingerprinting" a digital version. Fingerprinting converts the content of the work into a unique digital identification mark by applying an algorithm to selected features of that work.

Wrapping is the process where the license and the encrypted content itself are bundled in an additional mechanism, the result of which is the secure container that prevents unauthorized access throughout the life of the content.

DRM IN LIBRARIES

With e-books and journals that are available in electronic form, there are a number of databases that libraries are now routinely licensing that have embedded DRM systems that can be configured to library options based on the licensing fee that the library pays. For example, Figure 6-3 shows a screen capture of a FirstSearch result when the article is owned by the local library.

Figure 6-3: OCLC First Search DRM-I: Periodical Owned by Local Library

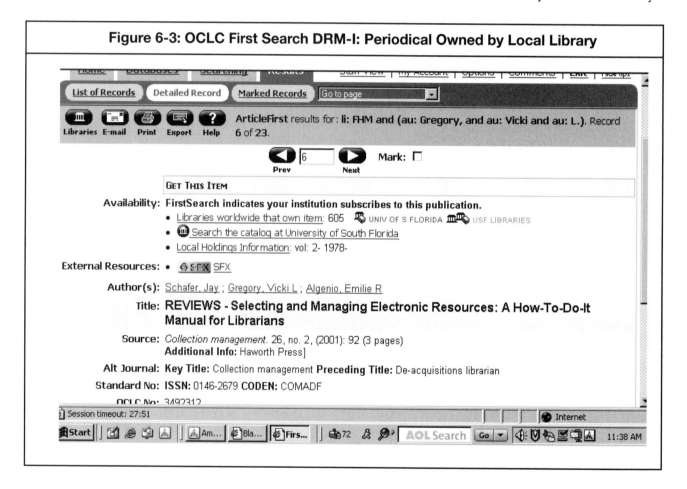

The user can find the article through the FirstSearch database, but once this particular article is selected, the DRM systems send the user back to the local library where it is owned with options for searching the local catalog. In this case the library has licensed the right for users to receive full-text e-mail delivery only in the case where the material is not already owned by the library.

Figure 6–4: Sample InfoTrack DRM-I: Document Delivery Option When Periodical Not Owned by Local Library

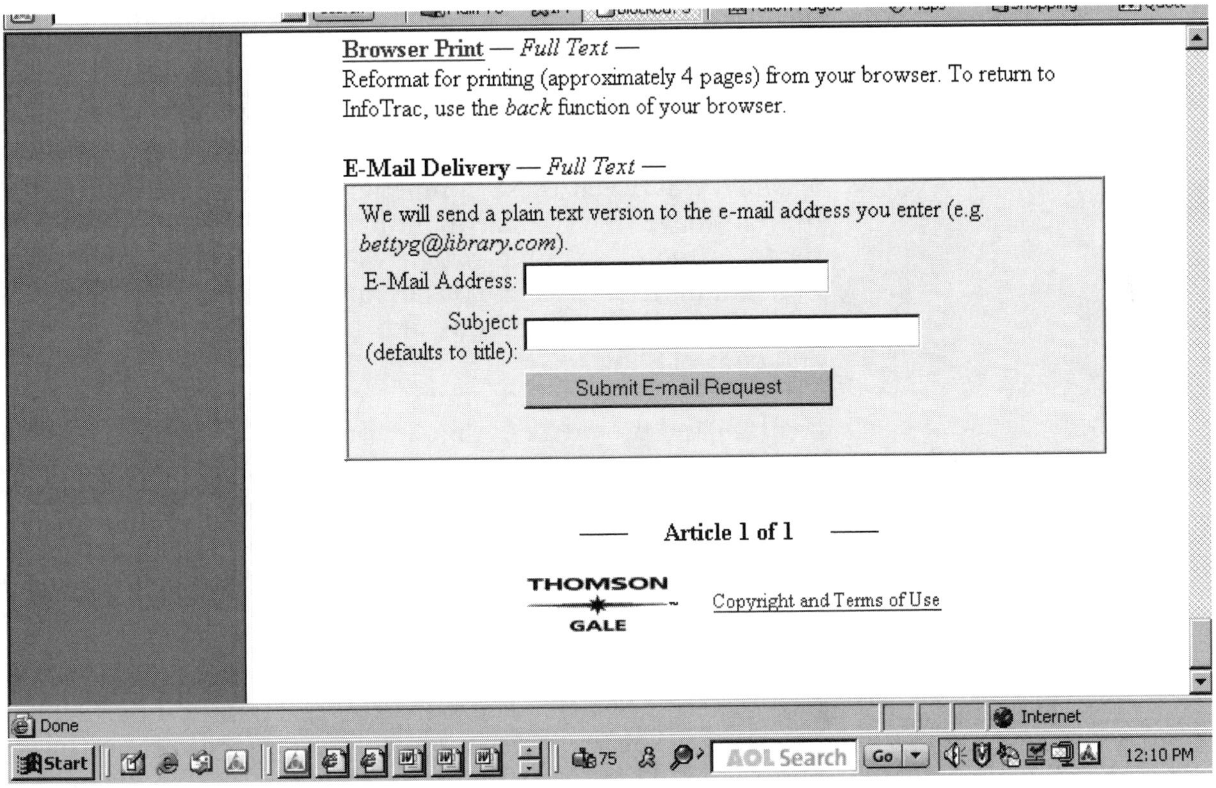

Figure 6-4 shows a screen capture of the delivery option for an article that is not owned by this same library. The DRM system determines when the searcher is authorized to receive full-text and when the items selected are not based on the holdings of the library that has licensed the database services.

CONCLUSION

"Fair use," as provided for in the U.S. copyright laws and taken advantage of by libraries in carrying out their core role as disseminators of information, has become increasingly and effectively eroded in the digital environment. Most librarians tend to believe strongly that traditional fair use rights must be as strongly maintained with regard to electronic resources as with print publications, and few would argue with this ideal; meanwhile, however, electronic publishers and other holders of copyright in respect of materials otherwise available electronically see a significant distinction. They base the distinction on the potential for essentially free transferability of limitless numbers of "perfect" electronic copies, unrestricted by the traditional print environment factors of copy quality degradation and the physical time and space restraints that manual copying typically imposed. Striking a balance between these competing interests is difficult, but librarians have to recognize that, increasingly, the purchase of and reliance upon electronic resources is moving away from traditional, familiar copyright considerations and fair use and first use concepts into the dangerous and unfamiliar world of licensing and contract law.

DRM systems are becoming increasingly common, allowing creators and providers of digital content to control access to and use of their products. The DRM approach differs from traditional copyright management in that it is proactive rather than reactive. DRM technologies restrict unauthorized use rather than from the start, rather than establishing a situation where a copyright holder can only respond after an infringement. It is the upfront nature of DRM that must concern librarians and users since it almost always involves a determination of fair use governed by algorithms rather than allowing a determination based upon a particular circumstance. For DRM technologies to be successful in the long run, the DRM industry will have to find a way to balance compensation to the rights holders with the rights of end-users to access and make fair use of digital information.

7 PRESERVATION ISSUES

Preservation issues are rising to the top of many librarians' thinking, in particular, where electronic journals are considered. In the rush to convert to electronic products and media, the traditional role of every library in preserving and archiving information for its particular community of users should not be forgotten. Libraries' users have generally depended on their librarians not only to select, purchase, organize, and make available currently needed resources, but also, as an inherent corollary to these actions, to save and preserve information that may have lasting value. Traditional library preservation strategies have therefore long been established for **physical** objects, but these strategies do not always neatly transfer to the preservation of a **digital** object. This is so because, in the past, libraries have been mainly concerned with taking steps to preserve the physical artifact (or a photocopied or microfilmed facsimile of the physical artifact) that contains the specific information desired, rather than preserving the information itself.

Preservation of digital materials is an increasingly important issue for research, development, and discussion, with the general perception being that preservation of digital objects is more problematic than with print or other formats. As more and more materials are available only in digital format with no hard-copy format to be preserved, digital preservation becomes an imperative issue for librarians and future users of such materials.

It was traditionally assumed that if a publication had been printed on long-life, acid-free paper, and if reasonable environmental conditions for its storage were maintained, access to the information could continue for an essentially indefinite period, or at least for quite a long time. This was work that was often well done—the oldest printed Gutenberg Bibles still in existence remain readable today, if not exactly easily usable in the sense of unrestricted access to the original. It is only relatively recently in library history that the format (electronic or digital) of materials has, however, become problematic for the preservation for future use of the information contained in those formats. The LOCKSS (Lots of Copies Keep Stuff Safe) model of creating multiple, geographically distant archives of digital materials is becoming increasingly an accepted one by publishers and librarians (*lockss.stanford.edu*)

Although libraries have always needed to take steps to deselect or weed their collections of unneeded, out-of-date, duplicative, or otherwise no longer useful books and serials, this process has almost always been accomplished (barring natural disasters, fires,

"Physical archives can lie forgotten for centuries in attics and storerooms and still be recoverable. Digital information is less forgiving."
—William Y. Arms, *Digital Libraries* (Cambridge, Mass.: MIT Press, 2000).

or other accidents) through a conscious and usually carefully considered decision on the part of librarians. However, electronic products open up the unhappy specter of the unconscious discarding, in effect, of the information itself through the outdating and obsolescence of the resource medium. For instance, if you purchase a serial on CD-ROM today, how certain are you, or can you be, that you will be able to access the material in its issues in the year 2020, or even two years from now? If you purchase Web access to that same serial, what happens if you drop the subscription next year, or if the company that provides you with access is bought out by another vendor that subsequently changes its access policies in ways incompatible with your systems or policies, or provides continued access only at significantly increased cost? If you decide to preserve a Web site, do you also have to preserve all the links made from that page if it is to be truly useful? If so, where do you stop? These issues are not only for research libraries; they are matters of concern for every library.

Possibly digital preservation's most recent development is the shift from large, project-based imaging initiatives to the digitization of more everyday items. This is similar to the earlier print preservation efforts that initially centered upon great collections, finally devolving into efforts to preserve deteriorating materials as they are found. This trend to digitize deteriorating materials is a new one that is not widespread, but, given the libraries such as at the University of Michigan who are now participating in such a project, it is likely to become more widespread in the future.

Self-publishing, which was once a tiny percentage of materials in the print world, has become a mass producer of information on the Web. "Born digital" materials are becoming increasingly ephemeral and thus a problem for preservationists for many of the reasons delineated in the following discussion.

IS DIGITIZED INFORMATION PRESERVED (OR PRESERVABLE) INFORMATION?

Digital preservation involves both born-digital and digitized documents. Born-digital documents are those that were initially created using some form of digital technology. Digital preservation of these kinds of materials is necessary to maintain their authenticity, reliability, and accessibility. Although sometimes the layman may think of digital information as being potentially preserved for eternity, it is becoming clear that at the present this is certainly not the case. Electronic formats keep changing, and unless the information contained in the older formats is constantly transferred to the newer mediums, it can and will likely quickly become lost. For example, locating today a new or refurbished $5^1/_4$-inch floppy drive (for which compatible disks were the predominant storage format for most microcomputer users a mere ten years ago) in order to read documents stored in that format is already more and more difficult. For those who have data on the even older 8-inch diskettes, accessing and moving the information contained on them to a current format remains a doable proposition, but it is both expensive and labor-intensive. As $3^1/_2$-inch diskette drives disappear from new computers to be replaced by CD or DVD drives and flash card drives and drives for other smaller media, soon what was the currency of portable data storage will also become inaccessible on most new computers. Even as august a body as the National Archives finds itself constantly on the search for, or even attempting to build from scratch, some older pieces of technology or equipment so that the Archives can transfer information from an obsolete format to a new one. It has become clear that the preservation of digital information requires both the financial wherewithal and a firm commitment to migrating data from one format or medium to another so as to ensure that the data can continue to be read. Figure 7-1 lists examples of obsolete media.

These same concerns also apply to those print documents that have been selected for digitization. Once they are in digital format, these materials also join the merry-go-round of materials needing to be kept in an up-to-date format. But even when a document (or information) is kept in a "readable" format, you must

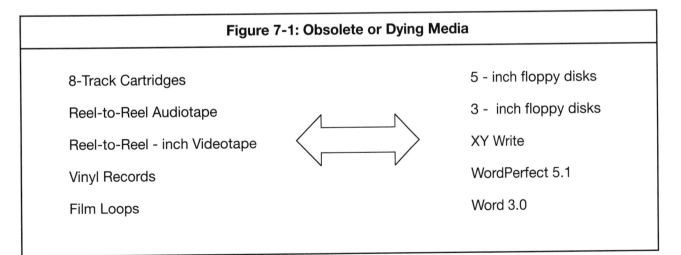

Figure 7-1: Obsolete or Dying Media

8-Track Cartridges	5 - inch floppy disks
Reel-to-Reel Audiotape	3 - inch floppy disks
Reel-to-Reel - inch Videotape	XY Write
Vinyl Records	WordPerfect 5.1
Film Loops	Word 3.0

also consider the durability of that format. At present the average life span of magnetic tape appears to be considerably less than that of most books, even those printed on acidic paper. Magnetic disk formats, while apparently somewhat better, have yet to meet the test of time, even assuming adequate protection from magnets, motors, and electric detection equipment; for optical disk formats, such as CD-ROMs, the life expectancies are apparently considerably longer, but there is no consensus on just how long, and there appear to be variations depending on the type of disk—estimates vary all the way from 10 to 100 years. But the life expectancies of electronic formats still appear paltry when compared to the expected lives of most printed materials.

Hardware format challenges are not the only ones lurking out there; the library must also be concerned about the software used to generate the documents themselves. In 1989, the latest in word-processing software included such now extinct, or nearly so, programs as WordStar and XyWrite. Can we be positive that ten years from now we will have the software available to read or convert a document produced using one of today's standard word-processing programs? It is clear that when we move away from standard ASCII text to formatted, word-processed documents, we necessarily become very dependent on having available the proper software to read the document, suggesting perhaps the need for a standard for electronic archives.

Today, to preserve information, many archives often convert their materials to a format that is not software-dependent or platform-dependent. Such formats are mainly pure ASCII texts, which are easy to save, but which lack the benefits of fancy fonts, bold-faced and italicized text, justification, and so on. Today, this approach seems the best, but it is an expensive one without any guarantees. After all, what future does ASCII have?

Another important consideration to keep in mind is that, unlike the situation with print materials, where good fortune often plays a crucial part in long-term preservation, there is no salvation in just doing nothing; electronic materials will be preserved and usable in the future only if positive action is taken on a current basis. In the past, many printed sources were saved by serendipity—that is, they just happened to survive on someone's bookshelf or in some library's otherwise unused storage area. In addition to depending on the life span of the material or medium on which they reside (magnetic tape, optical disk, and so forth), the "life" of electronic materials also depends on having available the hardware to run or play the physical medium on which the information is stored. As stated earlier, electronic information presently requires seemingly constant migration from one

A dim archive is one in which the titles are processed in a minimal manner and stored remotely in such a way that they could be recalled only if necessary. In contrast a dark archive is one in which materials are stored but used only as backups in a worst case scenario.

—University of California/ Stanford Government Information Librarians Group Minutes. [Online] March 20, 2003 Available: *http://www.library.ucla. edu/ucgils/March%2020 _rev.doc.*

format to another in order to keep up with the advances that are being made in both software and hardware.

Some libraries are beginning to create "dim" archives of print copies of journals that they are primarily acquiring in electronic form. The idea behind a dim archive is that the materials in it are only used in cases where the electronic version is no longer available. Materials in a dim archive are not fully processed, nor are they arranged for public access. They are simply being held in waiting in the event the primary, electronic version is no longer available. A few libraries have created "dark" archives where the materials are only to be used in a worst case scenario.

Another important issue is the sheer ephemeral nature of a large percentage of digital information. It may change or simply disappear before it can be captured and preserved. Print archives now contain the papers of individuals and authors that allow historians or literary scholars to trace the development of a work through its many drafts. In the electronic age, those drafts are likely not saved but simply written over by the latest version of the text.

Librarians simply cannot ignore the problem. Generally, libraries are seen as having collections of items that are deemed to be of lasting importance rather than items of an ephemeral nature. Therefore, to meet this expectation libraries must be able to access permanent archives of information that are available only in electronic form. In searching for a solution, librarians are justifiably reluctant to depend on commercial vendors to archive their materials, and they must therefore make the necessary commitment to move with the technology so as not to be left with something like the equivalent of an 8-track audiotape cartridge archive. A March 1998 statement of the International Coalition of Library Consortia (ICLC) argues that libraries, if they are to meet their typical preservation and collection mandates, must be able to purchase or license information perpetually, and not just temporarily license the electronic information they collect, so that libraries will retain control over the preservation of the information contained in the media; and this control necessarily includes the right to make backup copies. The problem is exacerbated when information is accessed only remotely, and the ICLC also argues that this type of provider should not be used unless there is some form of guarantee the information will be perpetually available.

WHO SHOULD ARCHIVE AN ELECTRONIC INFORMATION RESOURCE?

There are several possible answers to the question of who should archive electronic materials.

PUBLISHER OR VENDOR/AGGREGATOR

Many publishers do currently attempt to archive their electronic publications, but the problem seen by many in the library profession is that most such publishers make no commitment regarding the permanence of their archives. When it is no longer commercially profitable to do so, it appears unlikely that publishers will continue to make and maintain archives of their electronic materials. Librarians also worry that a publisher may go out of business or be sold to another company that decides that it is no longer in its financial interest to continue the archival arrangements of the first company. To make matters worse, even fewer publishers have indicated a commitment to moving their materials to current formats as needed for their preservation. Librarians in academic and research libraries strive to purchase materials for permanent retention, so preservation and archival issues are extremely important to them; depending on the publisher, however, the safeguards that may be in place will likely not be sufficient for a library's needs.

Some good approaches do exist. One example of a vendor approach to preservation is OCLC's FirstSearch Electronic Collections Online, which offers to subscribers perpetual access to its electronic resources. Another is JSTOR, which was established in 1995 as an independent, not-for-profit organization, to provide academic libraries with back runs of important journals in electronic form. JSTOR has straightforward licenses with publishers and with subscribing institutions. By emphasizing back runs, JSTOR strives to avoid competing with publishers, whose principal revenues come from current subscriptions.

THE LIBRARY ITSELF

Traditionally, libraries have always done their own archiving, whether through binding journal issues or in microfilming certain resources. It is conceivable that, given the permission of the publisher for licensed items, libraries could archive many of their electronic materials as well. However, the library must then make the same commitment to keeping materials in a current and usable format, and, if done in every library, these activities would certainly be expensively duplicative on numerous occasions. Librarians would doubtless feel the "safest" or most comfortable with this solution, but it is probably not a cost-effective approach to a general problem and it does not seem to be the method chosen by most libraries at this time. The one exception appears to be for materials produced locally, which many libraries do archive on the basis that they will likely be the sole source for these items in the future. A few libraries have begun creating dim or dark archives of their journals, so that in a worst case scenario, they will have access to a print copy of the journal if the electronic one is no longer accessible.

COOPERATIVE ARRANGEMENTS

As libraries have done with shared online cataloging for years, a cooperative arrangement could be worked out to preserve electronic resources, and this seems a most desirable approach. One suggestion currently making the rounds is that publishers could provide for a nonprofit organization, which would enjoy the right to archive and convey materials as needed and make particular titles and volumes available to libraries that held a valid subscription or had once held a subscription for the particular title and volume. A number of efforts are under way along these lines. For example, the Committee on Institutional Cooperation's Electronic Journal Collection is an effort by the major academic libraries in the United States both to archive and to offer access to freely available electronic journals. An additional example of a consortial approach by academic libraries is JSTOR, which provides for archiving of electronic journals for a fee.

WHO SHOULD BE CONCERNED WITH PRESERVATION ISSUES?

When reviewing the practical, how-we-did-it-well library literature dealing with electronic resources, it is obvious that a good many libraries have determined, whether consciously or by default, that preservation of electronic format materials may not be a matter for their concern. Preservation issues are simply not a part of their checklists of points to consider when purchasing or licensing an electronic resource. In some cases, it has been baldly stated that preservation issues were not of concern to that particular library when selecting materials. But it is clear that other libraries are obviously very concerned with such issues, even if they do not have answers for all the preservation issues that are necessarily raised.

This is an area where no library can be a self-sufficient island. Some type of cooperation and "unitary" concern is necessary if vendors and publishers are to make significant contributions to ensuring continued access to electronic materials. If the library community is deemed unconcerned, then the vendors and publishers obviously will not commit significant corporate dollars to ensure that their materials are in fact available in perpetuity. Also, libraries may need to follow the lead of a few cooperative efforts that have begun forming to work actively toward the preservation of electronic resources. Currently these efforts are mostly in the area of electronic serials, but that area of concern can be expected to widen in the near future.

Is this an issue only for research libraries? Although research libraries are naturally the ones most likely to be able and motivated to commit resources to cooperative preservation efforts, it is really a matter of concern for all libraries. Many smaller libraries currently rely on being able to borrow through interlibrary loan many specialized materials from a local academic or research library. What if that library that you have always depended on does not have hard-copy access to the material or, by the terms of a licensing agreement, cannot even loan you the material, much less print or copy any of it for your use? Preservation concerns involving electronic resources are properly the concern for all libraries and only by indicating that concern when you purchase or license materials can you help to ensure that the electronic materials will continue to be accessible.

INSTITUTIONAL REPOSITORIES FOR ACCESS AND PRESERVATION

In today's world, there are ever increasing resources available in digital format, not all of which are easily published in print format as they may contain multimedia elements that are not conducive to publication in a book or journal. Some journal articles may also have extensive data sets associated with them that are not reproducible in print format. For this information to be available for people to obtain and use, it has to be located somewhere, and institutional repositories are increasingly the answer to the question of access and preservation of these materials. Institutional repositories serve as digital warehouses for materials written by faculty of a particular institution or authors in a particular geographic area or a particular corporation, etc. In contrast to the dim archive, the institutional repository is holding digital materials while the dim archive is a repository of print materials.

A given institutional repository does not necessarily have to be for use of members of just one institution or for materials from one institution. Consortial repositories exist for a number of independent institutions which collaborate and pool their resources. In this case, the various member libraries or other organizations can all input and access all the materials.

Although a repository can preserve, and make accessible, materials produced in an institution or consortium, at the same time an individual repository forms a part of an international system of distributed, interoperable repositories available through the Web. Thus, the repositories provide a foundation for a new model of publishing centered on the author rather than on the publisher.

For librarians who are interested in setting up an institutional repository, there is open source software available to you. The source code for DSpace™ (*libraries.mit.edu/dspace-mit/technology/download.html*) is available for downloading as well as documentation and FAQs. At the Massachusetts Institute of Technology (MIT), the institutional repository is subdivided into collections by departments or individuals. Smaller libraries need not construct such an elaborate repository, but the software allows a range of options to customize a digital repository that is right for your institution.

DSpace is also designed to support a federation of institutional repositories of institutions who adopt this system. The DSpace project at MIT has envisioned multiple issues concerning access control, digital rights management, versioning, retrieval, faculty receptivity, community feedback, and flexible publishing capabilities. DSpace has also been designed to encourage author participation through ease of use. DSpace has also been designed to integrate with third-party software, allowing it to be coupled with other components.

CONCLUSION

Preservation concerns regarding electronic resources are far from being adequately resolved. For the foreseeable future, concerns are very real regarding continued hardware and software availability for reading the present generation of electronic materials. Access to licensed material involves both these issues and the legal right of future access to material that was previously licensed. We must ensure that the licenses that libraries sign today are not for limited access for a particular time period but that they allow for continued access to that same licensed material in the future. We must also have some protection from losing access to material when vendors are merged with larger companies or go out of business entirely.

Preservation efforts are currently being made in both digital and print repositories. Particularly within a consortium of libraries, the creation of dim archives of print materials is especially appealing for journals that are available in both print and electronic copies. Licensing access to electronic journals with the provision of one print copy being made to the consortium is more likely to ensure that there will be continuing access to the title.

To be secure in the knowledge of continued access in the future, cooperative arrangements between vendors and libraries are probably required. It would be naive in the extreme on the part of librarians to assume, once it is no longer profitable to maintain a resource, that the resource will somehow be maintained simply because future users might need access to it. Since for-profit businesses are indeed in business to turn a profit, cooperative arrangements in the nonprofit sector are probably required in order for perpetual access to be maintained. These kinds of arrangements, of course, will require the cooperation of vendors and publishers in order to allow libraries or special nonprofit organizations, such as JSTOR, to preserve the materials while allowing others to access those materials.

The movement toward the creation of institutional repositories may actively involve librarians in the preservation and access of local materials which are linked to similar resources in repositories around the globe.

8 THE FUTURE OF SELECTING AND MANAGING ELECTRONIC RESOURCES

THE SELECTION PROCESS

The proliferation over the past two decades and the public acceptance of (and indeed, in many cases, user preference for) electronic information resources have brought about dramatic changes in libraries, and these changes, while having a significant impact on all parts of the typical library, have had a truly profound effect on the work of collection development librarians. For many years, the explosive growth of publishing and the decline (in real dollars) of library budgets have resulted in increased pressure on library selectors not only to find the best resources for the library's users but also to find those resources at the lowest possible price.

The proliferation and corresponding popularity of electronic resources have only increased that pressure, but at the same time, technology has actually offered a way out of the problem through a more valid basis for "just-in-time" rather than "just-in-case" selection. The ability of a library to provide information not contained in physical form on its own shelves (whether through document delivery services, by online purchasing in general, and through telefacsimile, file transfers, or other forms of electronic delivery) means that any article or other resource needed by a client may be deliverable almost instantaneously, or at least within 24 to 72 hours—thereby significantly lessening the need for the many "just-in-case" purchases that most collection development librarians have traditionally felt were needed to meet their patron's anticipated or potential needs.

The importance of the selection process is reinforced by the traditional perception of many patrons that the library in some way vouches for the quality of the materials it collects, at least in the sense of the materials on the library's shelves being accurate representations of that which they purport to be. Much as we might from time to time hope to be able to disclaim connection with the content of every item in the materials made available in the library, the public does not usually see it that way, and this fact argues for even greater care in the selection of electronic resources, which are less easily controlled. Therefore, the growth of electronic resources will force librarians to become more collaborative in-house, with collection development librarians consulting with other librarians and specialists throughout the selection and implementation processes.

The expense of electronic resources is also bringing to the fore another type of collaboration—cooperative purchasing/licensing arrangements carried out through library consortiums—that must be utilized if soaring costs are to be rationalized with budgets. Thus, we can safely say that building a library collection today must necessarily be much more of a team process than it typically was in the past (when selectors worked pretty much in isolation within their respective specified subject areas). Electronic resources, coupled with the growth in interdisciplinary studies and interests, necessitates changing the selection process in many libraries from an individual decision approach to a team decision basis.

INTEGRATION OF ELECTRONIC RESOURCES

Integrating electronic resources, and the hardware/software needs that accompany them, into the process of collection development presents both an exciting challenge and a multifaceted problem. Beyond the traditional tasks of selection exist numerous management issues concerning budgets and personnel, and the arenas of copyright and preservation, as well as the need for improved organization, including bibliographic control, for access to information.

In many ways, digital products have proven to be something of a mixed blessing for libraries, at least at this point in time. Some of the most difficult problems they present have to do with the budgetary problems they create, and this at a time when operating costs are increasing across the board. Electronic resources, with their concurrent hardware needs and training requirements, are now being demanded by users, yet most library budgets typically cannot even keep pace with the recent inflation in book/serial/database pricing. The combination of sudden public popularity and shrinking library budgets in "real dollars" creates a stressful situation for many librarians juggling to meet user demands and needs in the best way possible.

Collection development policies have always provided a focus for a library's collection, and they are as essential for electronic resources as they have always been for traditional print materials. An integrated collection development policy that includes all types of resources is advocated as the best approach to the problem. Selection of electronic resources without the guidance of a collection development policy will usually lead to unfocused groupings of resources that may or may not fill the actual needs of the library's clients and that may or may not support the mission of the library as a whole. Because electronic resources are no longer frills to be treated almost as toys, but have become valid and necessary primary sources of information, they must be acquired in ways so as to fit into an overall collection plan.

Although, as we have seen, many of the basic traditional principles of collection development remain valid for electronic resources, methods of decision making and additional selection guidelines must be added to incorporate and reflect the differences between electronic and print resources. The old questions remain just as important in today's electronic environment as in the traditional print library:

- How should we select for collections and what do our users need?
- How do we make optimal use of limited budgets?
- How many serials and databases are sufficient and which particular ones are sufficient to meet our users' needs?
- How do we evaluate the existing collection and what can we do to determine its usefulness?

But selectors now often have to add to their choice of content the additional question of choice of format—print versus electronic, CD-ROM versus Web access, single-user access versus networked access for multiple users, individual subscription to a specific title versus a package of electronic titles from an aggregator. Another concern is how we determine what to purchase in this "just-in-time" information environment. Obviously, the library cannot wait for all materials to be requested before initiating access to them; but, on the other hand, it is considerably more difficult in today's environment to justify expenditures for items that are being or have been traditionally purchased only just in case they are needed.

Until very recently, the quality of access to information resources generally depended essentially on a user's physical proximity to a library and, of course, on the quality and quantity of the materials on that particular library's shelves. With users now demanding remote access to the library's electronic resources, more and more libraries are coming up with solutions to provide this service. These solutions have created additional problems that have to be considered and must be resolved, including which users should have access to which resources. Libraries must now also verify that their users are in fact persons who are permitted to have access to licensed, site-restricted, often Web-based information resources. Methods of vendor-allowed authentication may thus play an active role in the selection process, as many libraries do not wish to deal with resources that require the library to issue passwords to valid users; in many cases, even the method of IP source addressing does not meet the needs of the library's particular organization. Resources that use IP source addressing by requiring the library to set up a proxy server for remote users may also have to be taken into account.

Unfortunately, no single solution is universally correct, and different approaches are required by different organizations in order to meet local end-user needs most effectively. Client authentication and authorization issues are quickly becoming complex issues for libraries as they move into networked electronic resources and as they join together in group purchases of information resources.

A new resource that will undoubtedly bring additional changes into the way users want to access resources is the newly announced Google Scholar (*scholar.google.com*) that promises to provide easy access to electronic journals, institutional repositories, and other materials available in a digital format. Despite the rhetoric in response to the announcement, Google Scholar will not replace the library collection and the librarian, but rather it adds yet another source to the ever expanding repertoire of electronic resources.

"Whatever it does, Google Scholar will be wildly popular with students."
—Carol Tenopir, "Google in the Academic Library," *Library Journal* (February 1, 2005) [Online] Available *http://www.libraryjournal. com/article/CA498868.html*

HANDLING THE STRESS OF CHANGE

It seems that change has become a constant in the library environment in any number of ways, and change always produces some level of stress in any organization. But it must be remembered that stress is not always bad; it can be a consequence of good things as well as bad. Undertaking a new job or responsibility necessarily leads to stress, but hopefully it is a "good" kind of stress that helps the individual to learn and to grow in the job. In the library world, the introduction of technology has been related to many of those changes, and a relatively new, pithy term has even been devised for it—technostress.

There are a multitude of changes being driven by technology with which libraries today have to cope, and the increasing importance of electronic resources has forever changed the way libraries work. If we can find ways to fashion the electronic library out of the traditional print-based library, by using systematic procedures and policies, then libraries can continue to play in the future the valuable role they have always had; if not, users will, no doubt, find other means of obtaining what they need.

Librarians will also need to maintain a high degree of flexibility in this era of electronic resources. Old assumptions are constantly being challenged, and new ways of doing business are constantly being developed. As with early automation in the cataloging arena, organizational structures and reporting lines will need to change to accommodate team participation in the selection of electronic resources. Librarians may additionally find that their libraries are now members of multiple, and possibly overlapping and/or competing, consortiums set up to purchase needed or desired electronic resources at the lowest possible cost. Likewise, vendors will begin to find themselves in commercial competition with, or sometimes in partnership with, their closest business rivals to provide needed electronic resource packages for their library customers. Indeed, online publications produced by libraries themselves may place librarians in the position of either working cooperatively or competitively with commercial vendors.

Librarians should not, however, feel threatened by the challenges presented by electronic and networked information resources. If you are just beginning to add electronic resources to your library's collection, the combination of learning new technologies and managing decisions about choices for format and methods of access may at first seem formidable to you. However, by doing a little homework and visiting other libraries that may be a little further along in the process, plus visiting exhibitors at library conferences, participating in demonstrations by vendors, and combing through the professional literature, you should be well prepared to make the leap into the provision of electronic resources.

Being prepared to work in teams and to cooperate with other libraries is probably also essential. Librarians will need to call upon all their technical, service, professional, and human resource skills if they are to thrive in this new and rapidly changing environment.

SELECTED BIBLIOGRAPHY

The following items have been selected and are presented to provide the reader with additional information on major topics covered in this work. This is by no means an exhaustive bibliography on the subject, but it should provide some good places to get started.

GENERAL WORKS

Atkinson, Ross. "The Acquisitions Librarians as Change Agents in the Transition to the Electronic Library." *Library Resources and Technical Services* 36 (January 1997): 7–20.

Billings, Harold. "Library Collections and Distance Information: New Models of Collection Development for the 21st Century." *Journal of Library Administration* 24, nos. 1/2 (1996): 3–17.

Buckland, Michael. "What Will Collection Developers Do?" *Information Technology and Libraries* 14 (September 1995): 155–159.

Casserly, Mary F. "Developing a Concept of Collection for the Digital Age." *Portal: Libraries and the Academy* 2 (Oct. 2002): 577–587.

Crawford, Walt. *Being Analog: Creating Tomorrow's Libraries.* Chicago: American Library Association, 1999.

Demas, Samuel G. "What Will Collection Development Do?" *Collection Management* 22, nos. 3/4 (1998): 151–159.

Doyle, Greg. "Electronic Resources: Order Out of Chaos?" *OLA Quarterly* 4 (Fall 1998): 16–18.

Gorman, G. E., and Ruth H. Miller, eds. *Collection Development for the 21st Century: A Handbook for Librarians.* Westport, Conn.: Greenwood Press, 1997.

Gorman, Michael. "Ownership and Access: A New Idea of 'Collection.'" *College and Research Libraries News* 58 (July/August 1997): 498–499.

Grahame, Vicki, and Tim McAdam. SPEC Kit 282, *Managing Electronic Resources.* Annapolis Junction, Md.: Association of Research Libraries, 2004.

Harloe, Bart, and John M. Budd. "Collection Development and Scholarly Communication in the Era of Electronic Access." *Journal of Academic Librarianship* 20 (May 1994): 83–87.

Hitchingham, Eileen. "Collection Management in Light of Electronic Publishing." *Information Technology and Libraries* 15 (March 1996): 38–41.

Johnson, Peggy. *Fundamentals of Collection Development & Management.* Chicago: ALA, 2004.

Johnson, Peggy, and Bonnie MacEwan, eds. *Virtually Yours: Models for Managing Electronic Resources and Services.* Chicago: American Library Association, 1999.

Jordan, Jay. "New Directions in Electronic Collection Development." *Journal of Library Administration* 36, no. 3 (2002): 5–17.

Kovacs, Diane K. *Building Electronic Library Collections.* New York: Neal-Schuman, 2000.

Kovacs, Diane K. and Angela Elkordy. "Collection Development in Cyberspace: Building an Electronic Library Collection." *Library Hi Tech* 18, no. 4 (2000): 335–359.

Lancaster, F. W. "Collection Development in the Year 2025." In *Recruiting, Educating, and Training Librarians for Collection Development,* ed. Peggy Johnson and Sheila S. Intner, 215–229. Westport, Conn.: Greenwood Press, 1994.

Mouw, James. "Changing Roles in the Electronic Age—The Library Perspective." *Library Acquisitions: Practice and Theory* 22, no. 1 (1998): 15–21.

Nisonger, Thomas E. *Evaluation of Library Collections, Access and Electronic Resources: A Literature Guide and Annotated Bibliography.* Westport, CT: Libraries Unlimited, 2003.

Norman, O. Gene. "The Impact of Electronic Information Sources on Collection Development: A Survey of Current Practice." *Library Hi Tech* 15, nos. 1/2 (1997): 123–132.

Phillips, Linda L., and Sara R. Williams. "Collection Development Embraces the Digital Age: A Review of the Literature, 1997–2003." *Library Resources & Technical Services* 48 (Oct. 2004): 273–299.

Rowley, Gordon, and William K. Black "Consequences of Change: The Evolution of Collection Development." *Collection Building* 15, no. 2 (1996): 22–30.

Sankowski, Andrew. "Internet: Its Impact on Collection Development and the Curriculum." *Catholic Library World* 67 (March 1997): 16–18.

Schmidt, Karen A., ed. *Understanding the Business of Library Acquisitions.* 2d ed. Chicago: American Library Association, 1999.

Shreeves, Edward. "Selectors, Subject Knowledge, and Digital Collections." *Journal of Library Administration* 39, no. 4 (2003): 65–78.

Stolt, W. "Managing Electronic Resources: Public Service Considerations in a Technology Environment." *Collection Management* 21, no. 1 (1996): 17–28.

Stephens, Annabel L. *Public Library Collection Development in the Information Age.* New York: Haworth Press, 1998. Co-published as *The Acquisitions Librarian* 20, 1998.

Younger, Jennifer A. "From the Inside Out: An Organizational View of Electronic Resources and Collection Development." *Journal of Library Administration* 36 (Dec. 2002): 19–37.

COLLECTION DEVELOPMENT POLICIES

Case, Beau David. "Love's Labour Lost: The Failure of Traditional Selection Practice in the Acquisition of Humanities Electronic Texts." *Library Trends* 48 (Spring 2000): 729–747.

Demas, Samuel G., Peter McDonald, and Gregory Lawrence. "The Internet and Collection Development: Mainstreaming Selection of Internet Resources." *Library Resources and Technical Services* 39 (July 1995): 275–290.

Ferguson, Anthony W. "Interesting Problems Encountered on My Way to Writing an Electronic Information Selection Development Statement." *Against the Grain* 7 (April 1995): 16, 18–19, 90.

Hazen, Dan C. "Collection Development Policies in the Information Age." *College and Research Libraries* 56 (January 1995): 29–31.

Kabir, Abulfazal M. Fazle, ed. *Acquisition in Different and Special Subject Areas.* Binghamton, N.Y.: Haworth Press, 2004, Co-published as *The Acquisitions Librarian* 15, no. 29 (2004).

Mack, Daniel C., ed. *Collection Development Policies: New Directions for Changing Collections.* Binghamton, N.Y.: Haworth Press, 2004. Co-published as *The Acquisitions Librarian* 15, no. 30 (2004).

McGuigan, Glenn S., and Gary W. White. "Subject-Specific Policy Statements: A Rationale and Framework for Collection Development." *The Acquisitions Librarian* no. 30 (2003): 15–32.

Spohrer, James H. "The End of the American (Library) Dream: The Rise and Decline of the Collection Development Policy Statement at Berkeley." *The Acquisitions Librarian* no. 30 (2003): 33–47.

Strong, Rob. "A Collection Development Policy Incorporating Electronic Formats." *Journal of Interlibrary Loan, Document Delivery & Information Supply* 9 (1999): 53–64.

Vogel, Kristin D. "Integrating Electronic Resources into Collection Development Policies." *Collection Management* 2, no. 2 (1996): 65–76.

White, Gary, and Gregory Crawford. "Developing an Electronic Resources Collection Development Policy." *Collection Building* 16, no. 2 (1997): 53–57.

Wood, Richard J., and Frank Hoffmann. *Library Collection Development Policies: A Reference and Writers' Handbook.* Lanham, Md.: Scarecrow Press, 1996.

DIGITAL RIGHTS MANAGEMENT, COPYRIGHT AND LICENSING

Bielefield, Arlene, and Lawrence Cheeseman. *Interpreting and Negotiating Licensing Agreements*. New York: Neal-Schuman, 1999.

Carson, Bryan. "Legally Speaking." *Against the Grain* 11, (December 1999/January 2000): 54–58.

Cox, John. "Digital Rights Management: Old Hat or New Wrinkle?—Ready or not, DRM is Dramatically Altering Today's Publishing Landscape." *Against the Grain* 14 (November 2002): 22, 24, 26.

Coyle, Karen. "Rights Management and Digital Library Requirements." *Ariadne* 40 (July 2004). Available: *www.ariadne.ac.uk/issue40/coyle/*

Davis, Denise M. "Impact of Digital Rights Management on Access and Distribution of Intellectual Property in Libraries and Information Centers." *Technicalities* 20 (July/August 2000): 5–7.

Davis, Denise M., and Tim Lafferty. "Digital Rights Management: Implications for Libraries." *The Bottom Line: Managing Library Finances* 15, no. 1 (2002): 18–23.

Dusollier, Séverine. "Fair Use by Design in the European Copyright Directive of 2001." *Communications of the ACM* 46 (April 2003): 51–55.

Foroughi, Abbas, Marvin Albin, and Sharlett Gillard. "Digital Rights Management: A Delicate Balance Between Protection and Accessibility." *Journal of Information Science* 28, no. 5 (2002): 389–395.

Giavarra, Emanuella. Licensing Digital Resources: How to Avoid the Legal Pitfalls. 2nd ed. The Hague: European Bureau of Library, Information and Documentation Associations, 2001. Available: *www.eblida.org/ecup/docs/licensing.pdf*

Gregory, Vicki L. The Uniform Computer Information Transactions Act (UCITA): More Critical for Educators than Copyright Law?Åh In *Educational Media and Technology Yearbook* vol. 27 (Englewood, Colo.: 2002): 155–161.

Grove, Jeff. "Legal and Technological Efforts to Lock up Content Threaten Innovation." *Communications of the ACM* 46 (April 2003): 21–22.

Harris, Lesley Ellen. *Licensing Digital Content: A Practical Guide for Librarians*. Chicago: American Library Association, 2002.

Hoffmann, Gretchen McCord. *Copyright in Cyberspace: Questions and Answers for Librarians*. New York: Neal-Schuman, 2001.

Lessig, Lawrence. *The Future of Ideas: The Fate of the Commons in a Connected World*. New York: Random House, 2001.

Mulligan, Deirdre K., John Han, and Aaron J. Burstein. "How DRM-based Content Delivery Systems Disrupt Expectations of 'Personal Use.'" *Proceedings of the 2003 ACM Workshop on Digital Rights Management* (New York: ACM Press, 2003): 77–89.

Murray, Laura J. "Protecting Ourselves to Death: Canada, Copyright, and the Internet." *First Monday* 9 (October 2004). Available: *firstmonday.org/issues/issues9_10/murray/index.html*.

Okerson, Ann. "The LIBLICENSE Project and How It Grows." *D-Lib Magazine* 5 (September 1999): 8 pp. Available: *www.dlib.org/dlib/september99/okerson/09okerson.html*.

Pedley, Paul. "U.K. Copyright Law Leaves Much Open to Interpretation." *Information Outlook* 8 (November 2004): 35–36.

Samuelson, Pamela. "DRM {And, Or, VS.} the Law." *Communications of the ACM* 46 (April 2003): 41–45.

Worlock, David. "The Subtle Art of DRM." *Information World Review* (June 2001): 15.

ELECTRONIC JOURNALS

Ashcroft, Linda, and Colin Langdon. "Electronic Journals and University Library Collections." *Collection Building* 18, no. 3 (1999): 105–113.

Anderson, Rick. "A Sacred Cow Bites the Dust: Check-in Procedures to Monitor Electronic Journals at the University of Nevada, Reno.Åh *Library Journal* 127, no. 8 (May 1, 2002): 56.

Barnes, John H. "One Giant Leap, One Small Step: Continuing the Migration to Electronic Journals." *Library Trends* 45 (Winter 1997): 404–415.

Chadwell, Faye A., and Sara Brownmiller. "Heads Up: Confronting the Selection and Access Issues of Electronic Journals." *The Acquisitions Librarian* 21 (1999): 21–35.

Cochenour, Donnice. "CICNet's Electronic Journal Collection." *Serials Review* 22 (Spring 1996): 63–69.

Ellis, Kathryn D. "Acquiring Electronic Journals." *The Acquisitions Librarian* 21 (1999): 5–19.

Foster, Andrea L., Second Thoughts on 'Bundled' EJournals. *Chronicle of Higher Education* September 20, 2002. Available: *www.chronicle.com/free/v49/i04/04a03101.htm*.

Frazier, Kenneth. "The Librarians' Dilemma: Contemplating the Costs of the 'Big Deal,'" *D-Lib Magazine* 7, no. 3 (March 2001). Available: *www.dlib.org/dlib/march01/frazier/03frazier.html*.

Harter, Stephen P. "Accessing Electronic Journals and Other E-Publications: An Empirical Study." *College and Research Libraries* 57 (September 1996): 440–456.

Johns, Cecily. "Collection Management Strategies in a Digital Environment." *Serials Librarian* 43, no. 3 (2003): 83–87.

Kara, Bill, and Christine Stamison. "Keeping the Connection: Maintaining E-Journal Subscriptions" [Report of a program at the 2003 NASIG conference].Åh *The Serials Librarian* 46, no. 3/4 (2004): 309–313.

Kyrillidou, Martha. "Serials Trends Reflected in the ARL Statistics 2002–03." *ARL*, no. 234 (June 2004): 14–15.Available *www.arl.org/newsltr/234/serials.html*.

Lugg, Rick, and Ruth Fischer. "Agents in Place: Intermediaries in E-Journal Management: A White Paper." (October 2003) Available: *www.harrassowitz.de/top_resources/docs/AgentsInPlace20031024.pdf*.

Nisonger, Thomas E. "Electronic Journal Collection Management Issues." *Collection Building* 16, no. 2 (1997): 58–65.

Quinn, Brian. "The Impact of Aggregator Packages on Collection Management." *Collection Management* 25, no. 3 (2001): 53–74.

Tenopir, Carol. "Moving Toward Electronic Journals." *Library Journal* 125 (July 2000): 36–38.

Walters, William H. "Criteria for Replacing Print Journals with Online Journal Resources: The Importance of Sustainable Access." *Library Resources & Technical Services* 48 (October 2004): 300–304.

EVALUATION AND ASSESSMENT

Bertot, John Carlo, and Charles R. McClure. "Measuring Electronic Services in Public Libraries." *Public Libraries* 37 (May/June 1998): 176–180.

Breeding, Marshall. "Strategies for Measuring and Implementing E-use." *Library Technology Reports* 38 (May/June 2002): 1–68.

Clayton, Peter, and G. E. Gorman. "Updating Conspectus for a Digital Age." *Library Collections, Acquisitions & Technical Services* 26 (Autumn 2002): 253–258.

Cooke, Alison. *Neal-Schuman Authoritative Guide to Evaluating Information on the Internet.* New York: Neal-Schuman, 1999.

Emanuel, Michelle. "A Collection Evaluation in 150 Hours." *Collection Management* 27, nos. 3/4 (2002): 79–93.

International Coalition of Library Consortia. "Guidelines for Statistical Measures of Usage of Web-Based Indexed, Abstracted, and Full Text Resources." *Information Technology and Libraries* 17 (December 1998): 219–221.

Kirkwood, Hal P. "Beyond Evaluation: A Model for Cooperative Evaluation of Internet Resources." *Online* 22 (July/August 1998): 66–68.

McAbee, Sonja L. and William L. Hubbard. "The Current Reality of National Book Publishing Output and its Effect on Collection Assessment." *Collection Management* 28, no. 4 (2003): 67–78.

Pettijohn, Patricia, and Tina Neville, "Collection Development for Virtual Libraries" In Hanson, Ardis and Bruce Lubotsky Levin, (eds.) Building a Virtual Library. Hershey, Pa.: Idea Group Publishing (2003): 20–36.

Samson, Sue, Sebastian Derry, and Holly Eggleston. "Networked Resources, Assessment and Collection Development." *Journal of Academic Librarianship* 30 (Nov. 2004): 476–481.

Shepherd, Peter. "Keeping Count." *Library Journal* 128 (Jan. 15, 2003): 46–48.

Stemper, James A., and Janice M. Jaguszewski. "Usage Statistics for Electronic Journals: An Analysis of Local and Vendor Counts." *Collection Management* 28, no. 4 (2003): 3–22.

Summerfield, Mary, Carol Mandel, and Paul Kantor. "Perspectives on Scholarly Online Books: The Columbia University Online Books Evaluation Project." *Journal of Library Administration* 35, nos. 1 & 2 (2001): 61–82.

Svenningsen, Karen. "An Evaluation Model for Electronic Resources Utilizing Cost Analysis." *The Bottom Line: Managing Library Finances* 11 (1998): 18–23.

Van Epps, Amy S. "When Vendor Statistics are Not Enough: Determining Use of Electronic Databases." *Science & Technology Libraries* 21, nos. 1/2 (2001): 119–126.

ORGANIZATION AND ACCESS

Anderson, James D., and José Pérez-Carballo. *Information Retrieval Design: Principles and Options for Information Description, Organization, Display, and Access in Information Retrieval Databases, Digital Libraries, Catalogs, and Indexes.* St. Petersburg, Fl.: Ometeca Institute, 2005

Baker, Gayle, and Flora Shrode. "A Heuristic Approach to Selecting Delivery Mechanisms for Electronic Resources in Academic Libraries." *Journal of Library Administration* 26, nos. 3/4 (1999): 153–167.

Baldwin, Virginia. "Collection Development for the New Millennium—Evaluating, Selecting, Annotating, Organizing for Ease of Access, Reevaluating, and Updating Electronic Resources." *Collection Management* 25, nos. 1 & 2 (2000): 67–96.

Chandler, Adam, and Tim Jewell, "A Web Hub for Developing Administrative Metadata for Electronic Resource Management," 2001. Available: *www.library.cornell.edu/cts/elicensestudy/*

Digital Library Federation Electronic Resource Management Initiative, "Electronic Resources Management System Data Structure," Report of the DLF Electronic Resource Management Initiative, Appendix F. Draft 14 (November 2003). Available: *www.library.cornell.edu/cts/elicensestudy/dlfdeliverables/home.htm/ERMSDataStructure111403.doc*

Fisher, Rick, and Ruth Fischer. "Agents in Place: Intermediaries in E-Journal Management: A White Paper." (October 2003) Available: *www.harrassowitz.de/top_resources/docs/AgentsInPlace20031024.pdf.*

Glenn, Ariel, and David Millman. "Access Management of Web-Based Services." *D-Lib Magazine* (September 1998). Available: *www.dlib.org/dlib/September98/millman/09millman.html.*

Goerwitz, Richard. "Pass-Through Proxying as a Solution to the Off-Site Web-Access Problem." *D-Lib Magazine* (June 1998). Available: *www.dlib.org/dlib/June98/stg/06goerwitz.html.*

Godby, Carol Jean, Jeffery A. Young, and Eric Childress. "A Repository of Metadata Crosswalks." *D-Lib Magazine* 10, no. 12 (December 2004). Available: *www.dlib.org/dlib/december04/godby/12godby.html.*

Hill, Diane I., and Elaine L. Westbrook. *Metadata in Practice*. Chicago: American Library Association, 2004.

Heron, Susan, and Charles Gordon. "Cataloging and Metadata Issues for Electronic Resources" In Hanson, Ardis and Bruce Lubotsky Levin, (eds.) *Building A Virtual Library*. Hershey, Pa.: IDEA Group Publishing (2003): 78–94.

Heron, Susan J., and Ardis Hanson. "From Subject Gateways to Portals: The Role of Metadata in Accessing International Research." In Callaos, Nagib (ed.) Conference Proceedings Of The SCI 2003: The 7th World Multiconference On Systemics, Cybernetics, And Informatics. Orlando, Fl.: International Institute Of Informatics And Systemics, (2003): 529–533.

ISSN Manual: Cataloguing Part. Paris: ISSN International Centre, 2003

Lagoze, Carl, Herbert Van de Sompel, and Michael Nelson (eds.) Open Archives Initiative Protocol for Metadata Harvesting: *Protocol Version 2.0 of 2002–06–14*. Available: *www.openarchives.org/OAI/2.0/openarchivesprotocol.htm.Lugg.*

MacEwan, Bonnie J., and Mira Geffner. The Committee on Institutional Cooperation Electronic Journals Collection (CIC-EJC): a new model for library management of scholarly journals published on the Internet {computer file}.[E-serials archive on the World Wide Web.] *Public-Access Computer Systems Review (Online)* 7, no. 4 (1996) p. 5–15.

Miller, Dick R., and Kevin S. Clarke. *Putting XML to Work in the Library: Tools for Improving Access and Management.* Chicago: American Library Association, 2004.

Montgomery, Carol Hansen, and Donald W. King. ÅgComparing Library and User Related Costs of Print and Electronic Journal Collections. *D-Lib Magazine* 8, no. 10 (August 10, 2002). Available: *www.dlib.org/dlib/october02/montgomery/10montgomery.html.*

Newman, Gerald L. "Collection Development and Organization of Electronic Resources." *Collection Management* 25, nos. 1 & 2 (2000): 97–113.

Porter, G. Margaret, and Laura Bayard. "Including Web Sites in the Online Catalog: Implications for Cataloging, Collection Development, and Access." *Journal of Academic Librarianship* 25 (September 1999): 390–394.

Sadeh, Tamar, and Jenny Walker. "Library Portals: Toward the Semantic Web." *New Library World* 104, no. 1–2 (2003): 11–19. Available: *www.exlibrisgroup.com/resources/metalib/Library_portals_toward_the_semantic_Web.pdf.*

Streatfeild, R., and Darlene Hildebrandt. "Special Issues in the Sciences: The Case of Bibliographic Access." *The Journal of Academic Librarianship* 27, no. 5 (September 2001): 398–405.

The Unicode Consortium. *The Unicode Standard, Version 4.0.0, defined by: The Unicode Standard, Version 4.0.* Boston, MA: Addison-Wesley, 2003.

Young, Naomi Kietzke. "The Aggregator-Neutral Record: New Procedures for Cataloguing Continuing Resources." *The Serials Librarian* 45, no. 4 (2004): 37–42.

PRESERVATION

Brancolini, Kristine. "Selecting Research Collections for Digitization: Applying the Harvard Model." *Library Trends* 48 (Spring 2000): 783–798.

Brichford, Maynard, and William Maher. "Archival Issues in Network Electronic Publications." *Library Trends* 43 (Spring 1995): 701–712.

Butler, Meredith A. "Issues and Challenges of Archiving and Storing Digital Information: Preserving the Past for Future Scholars." *Journal of Library Administration* 24, no. 4 (1997): 61–79.

Chepesiuk, Ron. "JSTOR and Electronic Archiving." *American Libraries* 31 (Dec. 2000): 46–48.

Friedlander, Amy. "Digital Preservation Looks Forward: What We're Learning at the Library of Congress." *Information Outlook* 6 (Sept. 2002): 12–18.

Galloway, Patricia. "Preservation of Digital Objects." *Annual Review of Information Science and Technology* 38 (2004): 549–590.

Gertz, Janet. "Selecting for Preservation in the Digital Age." *Library Resources & Technical Services* 44 (April 2000): 97–104.

Hughes, Lorna M. *Digitizing Collections: Strategic Issues for the Information Manager.* London: Facet, 2004.

Hunter, Gregory S. *Preserving Digital Information.* New York: Neal-Schuman, 2000.

Jewell, Timothy D. *Selection and Presentation of Commercially Available Electronic Resources: Issues and Practices.* Digital Library Federation and Council on Library Resources, Washington, D.C., July 2000. Available *www.clir.org/pubs/reports/pub99/pub99.pdf.*

Kahn, Miriam B. *Protecting Your Library's Digital Resources: The Essential Guide to Planning and Preservation.* Chicago: American Library Association, 2004.

Kenney, Anne R., and Oya Y. Rieger. *Moving Theory into Practice: Digital Imaging for Libraries and Archives.* Mountain View, Calif.: Research Libraries Group, 2000.

Lynn, M. Stuart. "Digital Preservation and Access: Liberals and Conservatives." *Collection Management* 22, nos. 3/4 (1998): 55–63.

Marcum, Deanna. "Digital Archiving: Whose Responsibility Is It?" *College & Research Libraries News* 61 (Oct. 2000): 794–797.

Muir, Adrienne. "Digital Preservation: Awareness, Responsibility and Rights Issues." *Journal of Information Science* 30, no. 1 (2004): 73–92.

Smith, Abby. "Why Digitize?" Washington, D.C.: Council of Library Resources, 1999. Available: *www.clir.org/pubs/reports/pub80-smith/pub80.html*

Stanford University. LOCKSS (Lots of Copies Keep Stuff Safe). Available: *lockss.stanford.edu*

Teper, Thomas H. "Current and Emerging Challenges for the Future of Library and Archival Preservation." *Library Resources & Technical Resources* 49 (January 2005): 32–39.

Warner, Dorothy. "Why Do We Need to Keep This in Print? It's on the Web—A Review of Electronic Archiving Issues and Problems." *Progressive Librarian* 19 (Spring 2002): 47–64.

Yakel, Elizabeth. "Digital Preservation." *Annual Review of Information Science and Technology* 35 (2001): 337–378.

SELECTION

Balas, Janet I. "Developing Library Collections in a Wired World." *Computers in Libraries* 20 (June 2000): 61–63.

Davis, Trisha L. "The Evolution of Selection Activities for Electronic Resources." *Library Trends* 45 (Winter 1997): 391–403.

Hahn, Karla L., and Lila A. Faulkner. "Evaluative Usage-based Metrics for the Selection of E-journals. *College & Research Libraries* 63 (May 2002): 215–227.

Holleman, Curt. "Electronic Resources: Are Basic Criteria for the Selection of Materials Changing?" *Library Trends* 48 (Spring 2000): 694–710.

International Coalition of Library Consortia. "Statement of Current Perspective and Preferred Practices for the Selection and Purchase of Electronic Information." *Information Technology and Libraries* 17 (March 1998): 45–50.

Johnson, Peggy. "Selecting Electronic Resources: Developing a Local Decision-Making Matrix." *Cataloging and Classification Quarterly* 22, nos. 3/4 (1996): 9–24.

Johnson, Qiana. "User Preference in Formats of Print and Electronic Journals." *Collection Building* 23, no. 2 (2004): 73–77.

Kovacs, Diane. *Building Electronic Library Collections: The Essential Guide to Selection Criteria and Core Subject Collections.* New York: Neal-Schuman, 2000.

McGinnis, Suzan, and Jan H. Kemp. "The Electronic Resources Group: Using the Cross-Functional Team Approach to the Challenge of Acquiring Electronic Resources." *Library Acquisitions: Practice and Theory* 22, no. 3 (1998): 295–301.

Metz, Paul. "Principles of Selection for Electronic Resources." *Library Trends* 48 (Spring 2000): 711–728.

Persons, Nancy A. "Collection Development in an Era of Full-Text and 'Package Deals.'" *Library Acquisitions: Practice and Theory* 22, no. 1 (1998): 59–62.

Pratt, Gregory F., Patrick Flannery, and Cassandra L. D. Perkins. "Guidelines for Internet Resource Selection." *College and Research Libraries News* 57 (March 1996): 134–135.

Stewart, Lou Ann. "Choosing between Print and Electronic Resources: The Selection Dilemma." *Reference Librarian* no. 71 (2000): 79–97.

Thornton, Gloria A. "Impact of Electronic Resources on Collection Development, the Roles of Librarians, and Library Consortia." *Library Trends* 48 (Spring 2000): 842–856.

Walters, William H., Samuel G. Demas, Linda Stewart, and Jennifer Weintraub. "Guidelines for Collecting Aggregations of Web Resources." *Information Technology and Libraries* 17 (September 1998): 157–160.

INDEX

ABOUT THE AUTHORS

VICKI L. GREGORY received an M.A. in History and an M.L.S. in Library Service from the University of Alabama and her Ph.D. in Communication, Library, and Information Studies from Rutgers, The State University of New Jersey. She is currently Professor in and Director of the School of Library and Information Science at the University of South Florida in Tampa, where she teaches courses in the areas of library networks, collection development, library automation, and technical services. Prior to beginning her library education career, she was the Head of Systems and Operations at the Auburn University at Montgomery Library. She is the author of numerous articles and is an active member of the Special Libraries Association, the American Society for Information Science, the American Library Association, the American Association for Higher Education, the Association for Library and Information Science Education, the Southeastern Library Association, and both the Florida and Alabama Library Associations.

ARDIS HANSON is Director of the Research Library at the Louis de la Parte Florida Mental Health Institute at the University of South Florida. Interested in the use of technology to enhance research, she has presented at the Symposium on 21st Century Teaching Technologies and Internet2, showing innovative software applications. She is an adjunct instructor in the School of Library and Information Science and the College of Public Health at USF. Ms. Hanson was a member of the USF Virtual Library Planning Committee, the Implementation Team, the Interface Design Project Group, and the Metadata Team. She is a co-editor of *Building a Virtual Library* (2003).